Pocket

BERLIN

TOP SIGHTS • LOCAL LIFE • MADE EASY

Andrea Schulte-Peevers

In This Book

QuickStart Guide

Your keys to understanding the city – we help you decide what to do and how to do it

Need to Know
Tips for a smooth trip

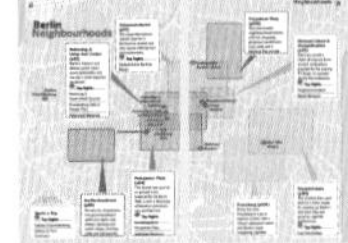

Neighbourhoods
What's where

Explore Berlin

The best things to see and do, neighbourhood by neighbourhood

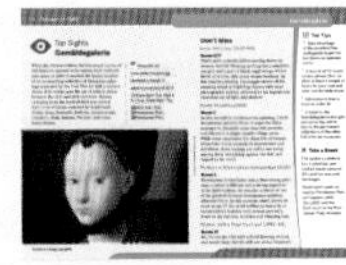

Top Sights
Make the most of your visit

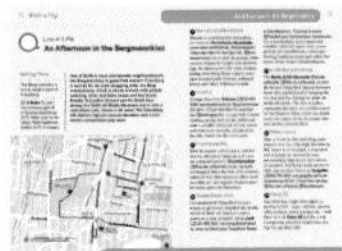

Local Life
The insider's city

The Best of Berlin

The city's highlights in handy lists to help you plan

Best Walks
See the city on foot

Berlin's Best...
The best experiences

Survival Guide

Tips and tricks for a seamless, hassle-free city experience

Getting Around
Travel like a local

Essential Information
Including where to stay

Our selection of the city's best places to eat, drink and experience:

Sights

Eating

Drinking

Entertainment

Shopping

These symbols give you the vital information for each listing:

- Telephone Numbers
- Opening Hours
- Parking
- Nonsmoking
- Internet Access
- Wi-Fi Access
- Vegetarian Selection
- English-Language Menu
- Family-Friendly
- Pet-Friendly
- Bus
- Ferry
- Metro
- S-Bahn
- U-Bahn
- Tram
- Train

Find each listing quickly on maps for each neighbourhood:

Bar Hemingway

16 Map p233, B2

Legend has it that Hemi self, wielding a machine ...rate this timber-pan ...ered bar during ... showpiece is a ...en by Papa ar ... town. Dress ...s.com; Hôtel Rit ...; 6.30pm-2a

Lonely Planet's Berlin

Lonely Planet Pocket Guides are designed to get you straight to the heart of the city.

Inside you'll find all the must-see sights, plus tips to make your visit to each one really memorable. We've split the city into easy-to-navigate neighbourhoods and provided clear maps so you'll find your way around with ease. Our expert authors have searched out the best of the city: walks, food, nightlife and shopping, to name a few. Because you want to explore, our 'Local Life' pages will take you to some of the most exciting areas to experience the real Berlin.

And of course you'll find all the practical tips you need for a smooth trip: itineraries for short visits, how to get around, and how much to tip the guy who serves you a drink at the end of a long day's exploration.

It's your guarantee of a really great experience.

Our Promise

You can trust our travel information because Lonely Planet authors visit the places we write about, each and every edition. We never accept freebies for positive coverage, so you can rely on us to tell it like it is.

QuickStart Guide 7

Explore Berlin 21

Worth a Trip:

The Best of Berlin 143

Berlin's Best Walks

Berlin's Best...

Survival Guide 173

QuickStart Guide

Welcome to Berlin

Berlin is a bon vivant, passionately feasting on the smorgasbord of life. A contagious energy permeates its cafes, bars and clubs, while indie boutiques and progressive restaurants compete for your time with world-class museums and striking landmarks that reflect the city's riveting history. Whether it's must-sees or aimless explorations, Berlin delivers it all in one exciting and memorable package.

Strandbar Mitte beach bar (p52)
TRAVELSTOCK44-JUERGEN HELD/GETTY IMAGES ©

Berlin Top Sights

Reichstag & Government Quarter (p24)

Views are mesmerising from the dazzling glass cupola atop the Reichstag, the seat of the German parliament and the stately focal point of the reunited country's government quarter.

Brandenburg Gate & Pariser Platz (p26)

Prussian emperors, Napoleon and Hitler have marched through this n classical royal city gate, once trappe east of the Berlin Wall and now a symbol of reunited Germany.

·rgamonmuseum (p42)

.lk in the footsteps of Greeks, mans and other ancient societies, ose monumental architecture, ›wcased in this museum, attests their astonishingly high levels of ilisation.

·denkstätte Berliner Mauer 74)

rather ironic that Berlin's biggest rist attraction no longer exists. To under the skin of the Berlin Wall stery, build a visit to this indoor- door memorial into your schedule.

Holocaust Memorial (p28)

Peter Eisenman poignantly captures the horror of the Nazi-inflicted Jewish mass murder with this vast undulating maze of tomb-like concrete plinths.

MAREMAGNUM/GETTY IMAGES ©

JEAN-PIERRE LESCOURRET/GETTY IMAGES ©

Neues Museum (p46)

Egyptian queen Nefertiti is the most famous resident at this top-ranked museum, beautifully reconstructed by David Chipperfield and also sheltering a feast of finds going back to prehistoric times.

Gemäldegalerie (p56)

Rembrandt is here, Caravaggio too. Botticelli, Rubens, Vermeer – need we say more? Your spirits will soar as you gaze upon centuries worth of masterpieces by Europe's art-world stars.

Potsdamer Platz (p60)

A post-reunification re-interpretation of Berlin's one-time equivalent of Times Square, the city's newest quarter shows off the talents of seminal architects of our times, including Renzo Piano and Helmut Jahn.

Jüdisches Museum (p62)

The 2000-year-old tale of Jews in Germany is a fascinating one, but just as powerful is the metaphorical language of Daniel Libeskind's extraordinary zinc-clad museum building.

East Side Gallery (p118)

On the longest surviving stretch of the Berlin Wall, more than a hundred international artists have translated their feelings about the barrier's collapse into powerful murals.

Schloss Charlottenburg (p96)

Prussian royals sure knew how to live it up, as you'll discover on a tour of the fancifully decorated living quarters of this grand palace attached to lushly landscaped gardens.

Schloss & Park Sanssouci (p138)

It's practically impossible not to be enchanted by this rambling palace ensemble dreamed up by King Frederick the Great, and merely a short train ride away in Potsdam.

Berlin Local Life

Insider tips to help you find the real ci

After checking out Berlin's top sights, experience what makes the city tick. Eclecti shopping strips, charismatic residential areas, chameleonesque neighbourhoods, neuron-destroying party quarters and even an antidote to 'boring Sundays' are all features that make up the Berliner's Berlin.

An Afternoon in the Bergmannkiez (p70)

- Eclectic shopping
- Urban oases

Wrapping around cafe-lined Bergmannstrasse, the Bergmannkiez (neighbourhood) is Kreuzberg's quieter and more bourgeois western section. After a spot of shopping, enjoy wide open spaces at an airport turned urban playground, contemplate the resilience of the human spirit at the Berlin Airlift Memorial and enjoy a beer on the hill that gave Kreuzberg its name.

Nosing Around Neukölln (p114)

- Vibrant creative scene
- Multicultural bar-hopping

Berlin's newest 'it' quarter is a shape-shifter, a dynamic and restless animal fed by an appetite for diversity and creativity. An exploration here is bound to be an eye-opener, perhaps even a glimpse into future trends. We can only provide suggestions on where to start, but give in to the local DIY spirit and you'll soon make your own discoveries.

Sundays Around the Mauerpark (p128)

- Flea market and karaoke
- Coffee culture

When it comes to the Mauerpark, we have to agree with the tens of thousands of locals and visitors: this is a great place to be on a Sunday, especially a sunny one. fabulous flea market, o rageous outdoor karaol barbecues and bands, a in a place once bifurca by the Berlin Wall, crea the ideal cocktail of fu and experience.

A Leisurely Saunter Through Schöneberg (p100)

- Cafe scene
- Indie boutiques

Often overshadowed by Kurfürstendamm to th west and Kreuzberg to the east, Schöneberg de serves its own spotligh It's a largely residentia but engagingly eclectic neighbourhood where greying suits rub shoul ders with party-hearty

Patrons enjoying alfresco drinks

ys, ex-hippies and
ırkish immigrants.
enty of street cafes
ovide perfect people-
atching perches.

otti Bar-Hop
›104)

3ars for all persuasions
Restorative fast-food joints

takes a nanosecond to
gure out that Berlin has
› shortage of libation
ations. By our estima-
on, the vibrantly gritty
ea around Kottbusser
›r U-Bahn station has
me of the city's best,
ıd all are conveniently
ıthin stumbling dis-
nce of each other. No
atter whether you're
e beer or cocktail type,
›u'll find a favourite
›oze burrow here.

Mauerpark Flea Market (p129)

MICHAEL TAYLOR/GETTY IMAGES ©

Other great places to experience the city like a local:

Berlin Day Planner

Day One

One day in Berlin? Follow this whirlwind itinerary to take in all the key sights. Book ahead for an early lift ride up to the dome of the **Reichstag** (p24), then snap a picture of the **Brandenburg Gate** (p26) before exploring the maze of the **Holocaust Memorial** (p28) and admiring the contemporary architecture of **Potsdamer Platz** (p60). See Berlin Wall remnants up close then contemplate Cold War madness at **Checkpoint Charlie** (p65).

Pop into the Friedrichstadtpassagen for a dose of retail therapy before a late lunch at **Augustiner am Gendarmenmarkt** (p36). Pick up a chocolate treat at **Fassbender & Rausch** (p39), then soak up the glory of **Gendarmenmarkt** (p32) on your way to Museum Island. Spend at least an hour marvelling at the antique treasures at the **Pergamonmuseum** (p42) until...beer o'clock! Head to the riverside **Strandbar Mitte** (p52).

Book ahead for a modern German dinner at **Katz Orange** (p81), earthy Italian at **Muret La Barba** (p83) or adventurous Vietnamese at **District Môt** (p82), wrapping up the night with drinks at **Butcher's** (p83) or dancing at **Clärchens Ballhaus** (p83).

Day Two

Kick off day two coming to grips with what life in Berlin was like when the Wall still stood, at the **Gedenkstätte Berliner Mauer** (p129). Hop the U-Bahn from Bernauer Strasse to Weinmeisterstrasse and take in a little boutique browsing around there and in t Hackesche Höfe.

Enjoy a Michelin-starred lunch at **Pauly Saal** (p81), then launch the afternoon's sightseeing with an audience with Queen Nefertiti and other ancient treasures at the **Neues Museum** (p46). Relax while letting the sights drift by on a one-hour **river cruise** (p52) around Museum Island. Next pop into the opuler **Berliner Dom** (p49), the court church of Prussian royals, whose city palace is beir resurrected opposite. Learn more about that at the **Humboldt-Box** (p145), which also a has nice cafe-cum-viewing-terrace

Excellent nearby dinner options include meat-free gourmet fare a trendy **Cookies Cream** (p36) or traditio al German at Berlin's oldest restaurant, **Zur Letzten Instanz** (p51).

ort on time?

've arranged Berlin's must-sees into these day-by-day itineraries to make sure u see the very best of the city in the time you have available.

ay Three

Start at **Schloss Charlottenburg** (p97), where the Neuer Flügel ew Wing) and the palace gardens musts. Take the U2 from Sophie-arlotte-Platz to Zoologischer Garten, editate on the futility of war at the **iser-Wilhelm-Gedächtniskirche** 90) and (assuming it's not Sunday) tisfy your shopping cravings along rfürstendamm. Drop by the **Bikini rlin** (p94) mall and then report to the **DeWe** (p95) food hall for lunch.

Dedicate part of the afternoon to the amazing Daniel Libeskind–signed **Jüdisches Museum** (p62), en go local on a stroll along **Berg-annstrasse** (p70), building in a cafe op and following your nostrils to the arheineke Markthalle to pick up some urmet treats. Then either amble east ng the scenic Landwehrkanal or take U-Bahn to Schönleinstrasse. Explore northern reaches of 'it' neighbour-od **Neukölln** (p114) on a DIY saunter fore deciding on a dinner spot.

Excellent dinner options are **Defne** (p108) for upmarket Turk-food and **Max und Moritz** (p108) for -sticking local fare. Continue into the ght on a bar-hop around **Kottbusser r** (p104).

Day Four

There's plenty more to do in Berlin proper, but we recommend you spend the better part of day four exploring the Unesco-honoured **Schloss & Park Sanssouci** (p139) in Potsdam, a 25-minute train ride from central Berlin. To avoid wait times, prebook online tickets for your preferred timeslot for visiting the park's main attraction, Schloss Sanssouci, a stunning rococo palace. Afterwards, explore the surrounding park and its many smaller palaces at leisure. The **Chinesisches Haus** (p139) exterior is a must-see.

Break for lunch at the park's **Drachenhaus** (p139), then continue your exploration before making your way back to Berlin in the mid-afternoon and heading to Prenzlauer Berg. Depending on your fatigue level, make a beeline to **Prater** (p135), Berlin's oldest beer garden, for a sundowner pint, or first spend an hour or so exploring the local designer boutiques along Kastanienallee.

Recommended dinner options in this charismatic 'hood include **Umami** (p133) for Vietnamese, **Frau Mittenmang** (p133) for creative international and **Zum Schusterjungen** (p134) for traditional German.

Need to Know

For more information, see Survival Guide (p174)

Currency
Euro (€)

Language
German (English widely spoken)

Visas
Not required for citizens of the EU, Australia, Canada, Israel, Japan, Switzerland, New Zealand and the USA (among others) for tourist stays of up to three months.

Money
ATMs are widespread. Cash is king in Berlin. ATM cards doubling as debit cards may also be accepted, but credit-card use is less common.

Mobile Phones
Mobile phones operate on GSM900/1800. Local SIM cards can be used in unlocked European and Australian phones. Most US multiband phones also work in Germany.

Time
Central European Time (GMT/UTC plus one hour). Daylight savings starts on the last Sunday in March and ends on the last Sunday in October.

Plugs & Adaptors
Two-pin plugs running at 230V/50Hz. Transformers needed for 110V appliances.

Tipping
Servers 10%, bartenders 5%, taxi drivers 10%, porters €1 to €2 per bag.

1 Before You Go

Your Daily Budget

Budget less than €80
- Dorm beds €10–20
- Self-catering or fast food
- Club cover charge €5–12

Midrange €80–200
- Private apartment or double €80–120
- Two-course dinner with wine €25–40
- Guided tour €10–15

Top end more than €200
- Nice apartment or double in top-end hote from €150
- Gourmet two-course dinner with wine €7(
- Cab rides €30–50

Useful Websites

Lonely Planet (www.lonelyplanet.com/berli Destination information, hotel bookings, traveller forum and more.

Visit Berlin (www.visitberlin.de) Official tour ist authority info.

Museumsportal (www.museumsportal-berlin.de) Gateway to the city's museums.

Resident Advisor (www.residentadvisor.ne Guide to parties and clubbing.

Advance Planning

Two to three months Book tickets for the Berliner Philharmonie, the Staatsoper, Sammlung Boros and top-flight events.

Up to one month Book online timeslot tickets for the Reichstag Dome, the Neues Museum and the Pergamonmuseum.

Up to two weeks Reserve a table at trendy restaurants, especially for weeken dinners.

2 Arriving in Berlin

st international visitors arrive at one of rlin's two airports, Tegel or Schönefeld (see w.berlin-airport.de). The Hauptbahnhof ain train station) is in the city centre, ZOB (central coach station) in the far stern city.

From Berlin-Tegel Airport

estination	Best Transport
exanderplatz	TXL express bus
urfürstendamm	X9 express bus or bus 109
reuzberg – ottbusser Tor/	X9/109 to Ernst-Reuter-Platz, then U8
otsdamer Platz	TXL to Brandenburg Gate, then S1, S2 or S25

From Berlin-Schönefeld Airport

estination	Best Transport
lexanderplatz	Airport-Express train (RB14 or RE7)
ahnhof Zoologi-cher Garten	Airport-Express train (RB14 or RE7)
reuzberg – ottbusser Tor	Airport-Express to Alexanderplatz, then U8
otsdamer Platz	Airport-Express to Friedrichstrasse, then S1, S2 or S25

From Hauptbahnhof

rlin's central train station is served by ses, trams, and U-Bahn and S-Bahn trains.

From ZOB (Central Coach ation)

e central coach station is a short walk from th U-Bahn and S-Bahn stations.

3 Getting Around

Berlin has an extensive, efficient and fairly reliable public transport system consisting of the U-Bahn (underground/subway), S-Bahn (light rail), buses and trams. One ticket is good for all forms of transport. Day passes are available. For trip planning, see www.bvg.de.

U U-Bahn

The most efficient way to travel. Operates 4am to 12.30am and all night Friday, Saturday and public holidays (all lines except the U4 and U55). From Sunday to Thursday, half-hourly night buses take over.

S S-Bahn

Not as frequent as U-Bahn trains but fewer stops and thus useful for longer distances. Same operating hours as the U-Bahn.

Bus

Slow but useful for sightseeing on the cheap. Most run frequently between 4.30am and 12.30am; half-hourly night buses run in the interim. MetroBuses (eg M1, M19) operate 24/7.

Tram

Only operate in the eastern districts. MetroTrams (M1, M2 etc) run 24/7.

Cycling

Great for exploring neighbourhoods. Designated bike lanes and rental stations are plentiful. Bikes are fine in designated U-Bahn and S-Bahn carriages.

Taxi

Can be hailed and are fairly inexpensive; avoid during rush hours.

Berlin Neighbourhoods

Reichstag & Unter den Linden (p22)

Berlin's historic hub delivers great views, iconic landmarks and the city's most beautiful boulevard.

Top Sights

- Reichstag & Government Quarter
- Brandenburg Gate & Pariser Platz
- Holocaust Memorial

Scheunenviertel (p72)

The maze-like historic Jewish Quarter is fashionista central and also teems with hip bars and restaurants.

Top Sights

- Gedenkstätte Berliner Mauer

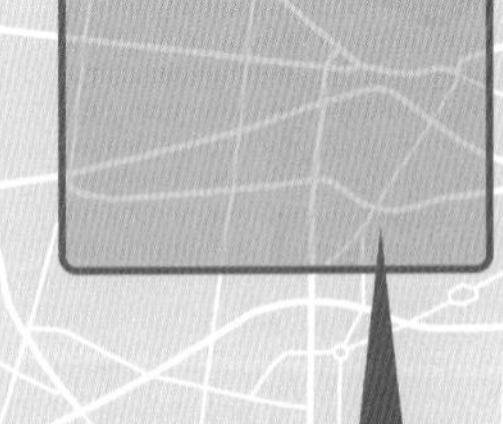

Potsdamer Platz (p54)

This brand-new quarter, on ground once bisected by the Berlin Wall, is now a showcase of fabulous contemporary architecture.

Top Sights

- Gemäldegalerie
- Potsdamer Platz
- Jüdisches Museum

Kurfürstendamm (p86)

Nirvana for shopaholics, this grand boulevard spills into idyllic side streets teeming with quaint shops, bustling cafes and restaurants.

Worth a Trip

Top Sights

- Schloss Charlottenburg
- Schloss & Park Sanssouci

Prenzlauer Berg (p126)
This charismatic neighbourhood entices with fun shopping, gorgeous townhouses, cosy cafes and a fabulous flea market.

Museum Island & Alexanderplatz (p40)
Gawk at a pirate's chest of treasure from ancient civilisations guarded by the soaring TV Tower on socialist-styled Alexanderplatz.

Top Sights

Pergamonmuseum

Neues Museum

Kreuzberg (p102)
Gritty but cool, Kreuzberg is a joy to explore on foot, with a vibrant restaurant scene and Berlin's most happening nightlife.

Friedrichshain (p116)
This student-flavoured district is tailor-made for soaking up Berlin's laid-back vibe and great for nightlife explorations.

Top Sights

East Side Gallery

Explore Berlin

Worth a Trip

Neue Synagoge (p78)
JUERGEN STUMPE/GETTY IMAGES ©

Explore

Reichstag & Unter den Linden

It's been burned, bombed, rebuilt, buttressed by the Berlin Wall, wrapped in fabric and, finally, adorned with a glass dome: this is the Reichstag, one of Berlin's most iconic buildings and seat of the German parliament (Bundestag). Nearby, the Brandenburg Gate gives way to Unter den Linden, Berlin's most elegant boulevard, which flaunts its Prussian pedigree with pride.

The Sights in a Day

Book an early timeslot for the lift ride to the **Reichstag dome** (p24) dome and get the lay of the land while meandering up its spiralling ramp. Back on solid ground, walk a few steps south to snap a classic picture of the **Brandenburg Gate** (p26), then get lost in the haunting maze of the **Holocaust Memorial** (p28). Ponder the source of such evil on the site of **Hitler's bunker** (p33) before strolling over to **Galeries Lafayette** (p39) and the Friedrichstadtpassagen for some retail therapy, followed by lunch at **Augustiner am Gendarmenmarkt** (p36).

Grab a sweet chocolate treat at **Fassbender & Rausch** (p39), take in the architectural harmony of **Gendarmenmarkt** (p32) and then follow Friedrichstrasse to Unter den Linden and continue north to the **Tränenpalast** (p32) to glean insight into the human toll the Berlin Wall took on citizens on both sides.

To compensate for the meaty lunch at Augustiner, enjoy a gourmet vegetarian dinner at **Cookies Cream** (p36), then report to **Bebel Bar** (p38) or **Tausend** (p37) for a nightcap or keep the night going on the dance floor at **Felix** (p38).

Top Sights

Best of Berlin

Eating

Shopping

Historical Sites

Getting There

Bus The 100 and TXL link the Reichstag with Alexanderplatz.

S-Bahn The S1, S2 and S25 stop at Friedrichstrasse and at Brandenburger Tor.

U-Bahn The U6 runs along Friedrichstrasse with a stop near Gendarmenmarkt (Französische Strasse).

Top Sights
Reichstag & Government Quarter

The nexus of German political power snuggles neatly into the Spreebogen, a horseshoe-shaped bend in the Spree River. The historic anchor of the federal government quarter is the glass-domed Reichstag, which once rubbed against the western side of the Berlin Wall. It now forms part of the Band des Bundes (Ribbon of Federal Buildings), a series of glass-and-concrete buildings that symbolically link the former East and West Berlin across the Spree. North of the river looms the solar-panelled Hauptbahnhof (central train station).

Map p30, C2

www.bundestag.de

Platz der Republik 1, Service Center: Scheidemannstrasse

Service Center 8am-8pm Apr-Oct, to 6pm Nov-Mar

100, S Bundestag, Hauptbahnhof, Brandenburger Tor

Reichstag

Don't Miss

Reichstag Building

The four corner towers and mighty facade with the bronze dedication 'Dem Deutschen Volke' (To the German People; added in 1916) are the only original sections of the 1894 Reichstag. Lord Norman Foster, the architectural mastermind of the building's post-reunification makeover, preserved only the historical shell and added the sparkling glass dome, Berlin's newest symbol.

Reichstag Dome

Whoever said the best things in life are free might have been thinking of the lift ride up to the rooftop of the Reichstag. Enjoy the knockout views, then pick up a free auto-activated audioguide and learn about the building, Berlin landmarks and the workings of the Bundestag while following the ramp spiralling up and around the dome's mirror-clad funnel.

Bundeskanzleramt

Germany's chancellor keeps his or her office in the H-shaped Federal Chancellery designed by Axel Schultes and Charlotte Frank. From Moltkebrücke bridge or the northern Spree River promenade you can best appreciate the circular openings that inspired the building's nickname, 'washing machine'. Eduardo Chillida's rusted-steel *Berlin* sculpture graces the forecourt.

Paul-Löbe-Haus

This vast glass-and-concrete building houses offices for the Bundestag's parliamentary committees. In a visual symbol of reunification, a double footbridge over the Spree links the building to the Marie-Elisabeth-Lüders-Haus, home to the parliamentary library.

Top Tips

- Compulsory reservations for visiting the Reichstag dome must be made online at www.bundestag.de. Early booking advised.
- Free multilingual audioguides are available on the roof terrace.
- Check the website for information on guided tours and on attending a plenary session or lecture on the workings of the Bundestag.

Take a Break

The **Dachgartenrestaurant Käfer** (☎030-2262 9933; mains €10-30; ⏰9am-4.30pm & 6.30pm-midnight) on the Reichstag roof terrace serves fancy fare; book at least two weeks in advance.

The nearest casual meal is at **Berlin Pavillon** (Map p30, C3; ☎030-2065 4737; www.berlin-pavillon.de; Scheidemannstrasse 1; mains €3-9; 🚌100, S Bundestag, Brandenburger Tor, U Brandenburger Tor), a cafeteria/beer garden on the edge of the Tiergarten.

Top Sights
Brandenburg Gate & Pariser Platz

A symbol of division during the Cold War, the landmark Brandenburg Gate (Brandenburger Tor) now epitomises German reunification and often serves as a photogenic backdrop for festivals, mega-concerts and New Year's Eve parties. It was in Athens' Acropolis that Carl Gotthard Langhans found inspiration for the elegant triumphal arch, completed in 1791 as the royal city gate. It stands sentinel over Pariser Platz, a harmoniously proportioned square once again framed by embassies and bank buildings, as it was during its 19th-century heyday.

Map p30, D3

Pariser Platz

admission free

24hr

S Brandenburger Tor, U Brandenburger Tor

Don't Miss

Quadriga

Crowning the Brandenburg Gate is Johann Gottfried Schadow's sculpture of the winged goddess of victory piloting a chariot drawn by four horses. After trouncing Prussia in 1806, Napoleon kidnapped and held her hostage in Paris until she was freed by a gallant Prussian general in 1815.

Hotel Adlon

A near-replica of the 1907 original, the **Adlon** (030-226 10; www.kempinski.com; Unter den Linden 77, Pariser Platz; r from €280;) is Berlin's poshest hotel. It reportedly inspired the 1932 movie *Grand Hotel*. Now called the Adlon Kempinksi, it's still a favourite haunt of the famous, powerful and eccentric. Remember Michael Jackson dangling his baby out the window? It happened at the Adlon.

Academy of Arts

The only building on Pariser Platz with a glass facade is the **Akademie der Künste** (Academy of Arts; 200 571 000; www.adk.de; Pariser Platz 4; admission varies, free 3-7pm Tue; exhibits 11am-7pm Tue-Sun), designed by Günter Behnisch. This is one of Berlin's oldest cultural institutions, founded by King Friedrich I in 1696 as the Prussian Academy of Arts, and now offers many free readings, lectures, workshops and exhibits.

DZ Bank

California-based deconstructivist Frank Gehry masterminded this **bank** (Pariser Platz 3; Brandenburger Tor), which packs a visual punch beyond those bland doors. You'll only get as far as the foyer (open weekdays) but can glimpse the glass-covered atrium with its bizarre free-form sculpture that's actually a conference room.

Top Tips

- Pick up maps and information at the tourist office in the gate's south wing.
- For a few quiet minutes, pop into the nondenominational meditation room in the gate's north wing.
- Sunset and dusk offer the best light conditions for picture-taking.
- Check out the schedule of exhibits, readings, lectures and workshops at the Academy of Arts (founded in 1696) on Pariser Platz.
- A free exhibition in the Brandenburger Tor U-Bahn station pinpoints milestones in the gate's history.

Take a Break

Head to the Hotel Adlon for coffee and cake, a light lunch or a classic afternoon tea.

At dinnertime, feast on vegetarian fare at Cookies Cream (p36).

Top Sights
Holocaust Memorial

It took 17 years of discussion, planning and construction, but on 10 May 2005 the Memorial to the Murdered Jews of Europe was officially dedicated. Colloquially known as the Holocaust Memorial, it's Germany's central memorial to the Nazi-planned genocide of the Third Reich. In a space the size of a football field, New York architect Peter Eisenman created 2711 sarcophagi-like stelae rising in sombre silence from undulating ground. You're free to access this labyrinth at any point and make your individual journey through it.

Map p30, D4

030-2639 4336

www.stiftung-denkmal.de

Cora-Berliner-Strasse 1

field 24hr; info centre 10am-7pm or 8pm

S Brandenburger Tor, Brandenburger Tor

Don't Miss

Field of Stelae

At first, Peter Eisenman's massive grid of concrete columns of equal size at various heights may seem austere and unemotional, but take time to feel the coolness of the stone and contemplate the interplay of light and shadow. Then plunge into this maze of narrow passageways and give yourself over to a metaphorical sense of disorientation, confusion and claustrophobia.

Ort der Information

If the memorial itself feels rather abstract, the information centre movingly lifts the veil of anonymity from the six million Holocaust victims. A graphic timeline of Jewish persecution during the Third Reich is followed by a series of rooms documenting the fates of individuals and families. Poignant and heart-wrenching, these exhibits will leave no one untouched.

Room of Names

In this darkened and most visceral room in the information centre, the names and years of birth and death of Jewish victims are projected onto all four walls while a solemn voice reads their short biographies. It takes almost seven years to commemorate all known victims in this fashion.

Homosexuellen-Denkmal

The Gay Memorial trains the spotlight on the tremendous persecution and suffering of Europe's gay community under the Nazis. Across from the Holocaust Memorial, it's a freestanding 4m-high off-kilter concrete cube designed by Danish-Norwegian artists (and Berlin residents) Michael Elmgreen and Ingar Dragset. A looped video plays through a warped, narrow window.

☑ Top Tips

- ▶ Free guided tours in English take place at 3pm on Saturday; German tours run at 3pm on Sunday.
- ▶ Last admission to the information centre is 45 minutes before closing.
- ▶ The memorial is at its moodiest (and most photogenic) when shadows are long, ie early morning or late in the day.
- ▶ Audioguides cost €4 for an adult or €2 for a concession.

Take a Break

The Roof (Map p30, D4; ☎030-2248 8570; www.welovecoffee.de; Cora-Berliner-Strasse 2; meals €3-10; ⏲11am-midnight; S Brandenburger Tor, Brandenburger Tor) is a good place to enjoy coffee and a light meal; its terrace has sweeping views of the Holocaust Memorial.

For a wide selection of eating and drinking options, take a short stroll down to Potsdamer Platz.

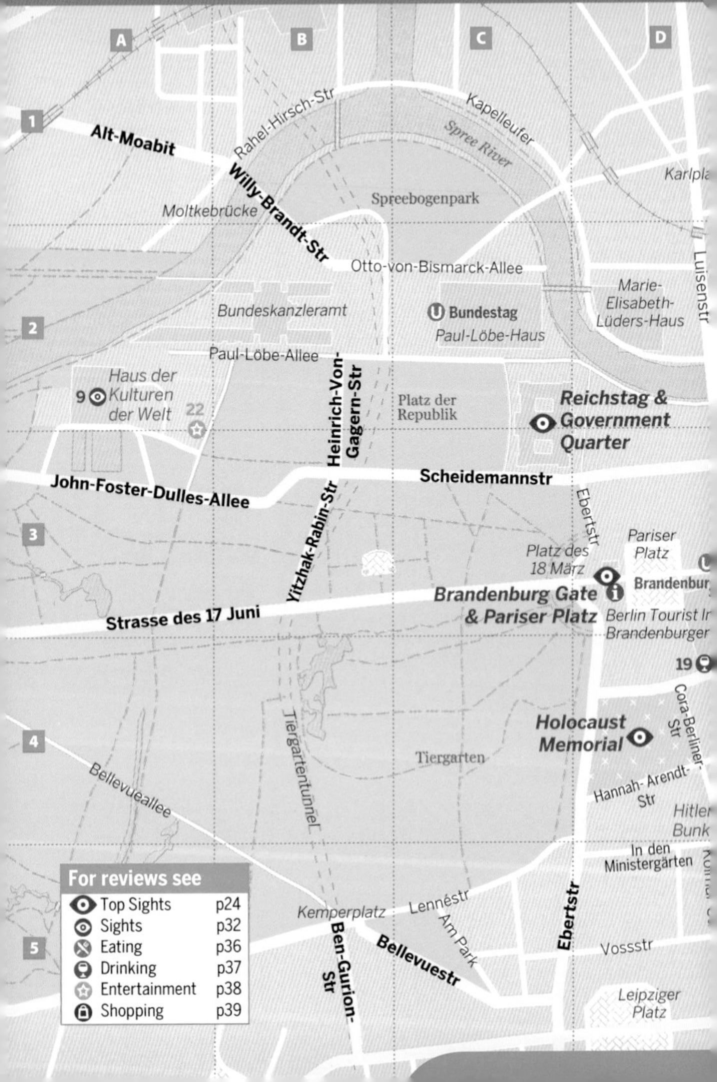

A B C D

1 2 3 4 5

Alt-Moabit
Rahel-Hirsch-Str
Kapelleufer
Spree River
Karlpla
Willy-Brandt-Str
Moltkebrücke
Spreebogenpark
Otto-von-Bismarck-Allee
Luisenstr
Marie-Elisabeth-Lüders-Haus
Bundeskanzleramt
Bundestag
Paul-Löbe-Haus
Paul-Löbe-Allee
Heinrich-Von-Gagern-Str
9 Haus der Kulturen der Welt
22
Platz der Republik
Reichstag & Government Quarter
John-Foster-Dulles-Allee
Scheidemannstr
Yitzhak-Rabin-Str
Ebertstr
Pariser Platz
Platz des 18 März
Brandenbur
Brandenburg Gate & Pariser Platz
Berlin Tourist In
Brandenburger
Strasse des 17 Juni
19
Cora-Berliner-Str
Holocaust Memorial
Tiergartentunnel
Tiergarten
Hannah-Arendt-Str
Bellevueallee
Hitler Bunk
In den Ministergärten
Kemperplatz
Lennéstr
Am Park
Ebertstr
Ben-Gurion-Str
Bellevuestr
Vossstr
Leipziger Platz

For reviews see

E
F
G
H
Johannisstr
Ziegelstr
Tucholskystr
Monbijoustr
Monbijouplatz
Monbijou Park
Albrechtstr
Bertolt-Brecht-Platz
Spree River
Am Weidendamm
Am Kupfergraben
17
Tränenpalast
16
3
Friedrichstr
21
Planckstr
Geschwister-Scholl-Str
MUSEUM ISLAND (MUSEUMSINSEL)
Spreekanal
Bahnhof Friedrichstr
Friedrichstr
Georgenstr
Reichstagufer
Bauhofstr
Am Zeughaus
Bodestr
Am Festungsgraben
Deutsches Historisches Museum
2
4
23
11
Mittelstr
Charlottenstr
Universitätsstr
Humboldt Universität
Neue Wache
6
Kunsthalle Deutsche Bank
Schlossbrücke
Unter den Linden
10
Deutsche Guggenheim
7
Bebelplatz
Oberwallstr
Behrenstr
18
Friedrichswerdersche Kirche
Friedrichstr
12
Französische Str
Kurstr
Französische Str
Glinkastr
25
14
Jägerstr
15
Mauerstr
Jägerstr
20
1
13
Gendarmenmarkt
Taubenstr
Hausvogteiplatz
Hausvogteiplatz
Niederwallstr
Taubenstr
Mohrenstr
Jerusalemer Str
Markgrafenstr
24
Mohrenstr
Wilhelmstr
Kronenstr
Stadtmitte
Leipziger Str
0
400 m
0
0.2 miles
1
2
3
4
5

Sights

Gendarmenmarkt

SQUARE

Berlin's most graceful square is bookended by the domed 18th-century German and French cathedrals and punctuated by a grandly porticoed concert hall, the Konzerthaus (p38). It was named for the Gens d'Armes, an 18th-century Prussian regiment consisting of French Huguenot immigrants whose story is chronicled in a museum inside the French cathedral. Climb the tower here for grand views of historic Berlin. (24hr; S Französische Strasse, Stadtmitte)

Deutsches Historisches Museum

MUSEUM

This engaging museum zeroes in on 1500 years of German history in all its gore and glory; not in a nutshell but on two floors of a Prussian-era armoury. Check out the Nazi globe, the pain-wrecked faces of dying warrior sculptures in the courtyard, and the temporary exhibits in the boldly modern annex designed by IM Pei. (030-203 040; www.dhm.de; Unter den Linden 2; adult/concession/under 18 yr €8/4/free; 10am-6pm; 100, 200, Alexanderplatz, Hackescher Markt)

Tränenpalast

MUSEUM

During the Cold War, tears flowed copiously in this glass-and-steel border-crossing pavilion where East Berliners had to bid adieu to family visiting from West Germany – hence its moniker 'Palace of Tears'. The exhibit uses original objects (including the claustrophobic passport control booths and a border auto-firing system),

Understand

The Reichstag in History

Germany's federal parliament building has witnessed many milestones in the country's history. After WWI, Philipp Scheidemann proclaimed the German Republic from one of its windows. The Reichstag fire in February 1933 allowed Adolf Hitler to blame the communists and helped catapult him to power. A dozen years later, victorious Red Army troops raised the Soviet flag on the bombed-out building, which stood damaged and empty on the western side of the Berlin Wall throughout the Cold War.

In the 1980s, megastars such as David Bowie, Pink Floyd and Michael Jackson performed concerts in front of the building. After the collapse of the Berlin Wall, reunification was enacted in the Reichstag in 1990. Five years later, it made headlines again when the artist couple Christo and Jeanne-Claude wrapped it in fabric. Lord Norman Foster began renovations shortly thereafter.

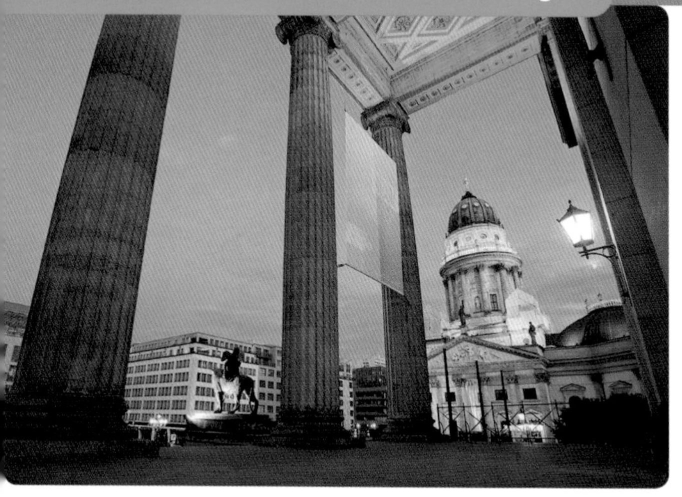

Gendarmenmarkt and Konzerthaus Berlin (p38)

photographs and historical footage to document the division's social impact on the daily lives of Germans on both sides of the border. (☎030-4677 7790; www.hdg.de; Reichstagufer 17; admission free; 9am-7pm Tue-Fri, 10am-6pm Sat & Sun; S Friedrichstrasse, Friedrichstrasse)

Neue Wache MEMORIAL

4 Map p30, H3

This columned, templelike neoclassical structure (1818) was Karl Friedrich Schinkel's first Berlin commission. Originally a Prussian royal guardhouse, it is now an antiwar memorial whose austere interior is dominated by Käthe Kollwitz' heart-wrenching sculpture of a mother cradling her dead soldier son. (Unter den Linden 4; admission free; 10am-6pm; 100, 200, TXL)

Hitler's Bunker HISTORIC SITE

5 Map p30, D4

Berlin was burning and Soviet tanks advancing relentlessly when Adolf Hitler committed suicide on 30 April 1945, alongside Eva Braun, his long-time female companion, hours after their marriage. Today, a parking lot covers the site, revealing its dark history only via an information panel with a diagram of the vast bunker network, construction data and the site's post-WWII history. (cnr In den Ministergärten & Gertrud-Kolmar-Strasse; 24hr; S Brandenburger Tor, Brandenburger Tor)

Understand

Berlin under the Swastika

The rise to power of Adolf Hitler and the NSDAP (Nazi Party) in January 1933 had instant and far-reaching consequences for all of Germany. Within three months, all non-Nazi parties, organisations and labour unions had been outlawed and many political opponents, intellectuals and artists detained without trial. Jews, of course, were a main target from the start but the horror escalated for them during the Kristallnacht pogroms on 9 November 1938, when Nazi thugs desecrated, burned and demolished synagogues and Jewish cemeteries, property and businesses across the country. Jews had begun to emigrate after 1933, but this event set off a stampede.

The fate of those Jews who stayed behind is well known: the systematic, bureaucratic and meticulously documented annihilation in death camps, mostly in Nazi-occupied territories in Eastern Europe. Sinti and Roma (gypsies), political opponents, priests, gays and habitual criminals were targeted as well. Of the roughly seven million people who were sent to concentration camps, only 500,000 survived.

The Battle of Berlin

With the Normandy invasion of June 1944, Allied troops arrived in formidable force on the European mainland, supported by unrelenting air raids on Berlin and most other German cities. The final Battle of Berlin began in mid-April 1945, with 1.5 million Soviet troops barrelling towards the city from the east. On 30 April, when the fighting reached the government quarter, Hitler and his long-time companion Eva Braun committed suicide in their bunker. As their bodies were burning, Red Army soldiers raised the Soviet flag above the Reichstag.

Defeat & Aftermath

The Battle of Berlin ended on 2 May, with Germany's unconditional surrender six days later. The fighting had taken an enormous toll on Berlin and its people. Much of the city lay in smouldering rubble and at least 125,000 Berliners had lost their lives. In July 1945, the leaders of the Allies met in Potsdam to carve up Germany and Berlin into four zones of occupation controlled by Britain, the USA, the USSR and France.

Kunsthalle Deutsche Bank

GALLERY

6 Map p30, G3

This small exhibition hall is a platform for contemporary art, especially from emerging art centres in Africa, China, India and South America. The three to four exhibits per year (often in cooperation with international museums like the Tate Modern) seek to push artistic boundaries and examine the effects of a globalised society. (030-202 0930; www.deutsche-bank-kunsthalle.de; Unter den Linden 13-15; adult/concession/child €4/3/free, free Mon; 10am-8pm; 100, 200, S Französische Strasse)

Bebelplatz

SQUARE, MEMORIAL

7 Map p30, G3

In 1933, books by Brecht, Mann, Marx and other 'subversives' went up in flames on this treeless square during the first full-blown public book burning, staged by the Nazi German Student League. Named for August Bebel, the cofounder of Germany's Social Democratic Party (SPD), it was first laid out in the 18th century under Frederick the Great. (24hr; 100, 200, TXL, S Hausvogteiplatz)

Madame Tussauds

MUSEUM

8 Map p30, E3

No celebrity in town to snare your stare? Don't fret: at this legendary wax museum the world's biggest pop stars, Hollywood legends, sports heroes and historical icons stand still – very still – for you to snap their picture. Sure, it's an expensive haven of kitsch and camp but where else can you have a candle-light dinner with George Clooney, play piano with Beethoven or test your IQ against Albert Einstein? Avoid wait times and save money by buying tickets online. (01806-545 800; www.madametussauds.com/berlin; Unter den Linden 74; adult/child 3-14yr €21/16; 10am-7pm Sep-Jul, 10am-8pm Aug, last admission 1hr before closing; 100, S Brandenburger Tor, Brandenburger Tor)

Haus der Kulturen der Welt

CULTURAL BUILDING

9 Map p30, A2

This highly respected cultural centre showcases contemporary non-European art, music, dance, literature, films and theatre, and also serves as a discussion forum on Zeitgeist-reflecting issues. The gravity-defying parabolic roof of Hugh Stubbins' extravagant building, designed as the American contribution to a 1957 architectural exhibition, is echoed by Henry Moore's sculpture *Butterfly* in the reflecting pool. (House of World Cultures; 030-397 870; www.hkw.de; John-Foster-Dulles-Allee 10; cost varies; exhibits 11am-7pm Wed-Mon; 100, S Bundestag, Hauptbahnhof)

Eating

Cookies Cream VEGETARIAN €€€

10 Map p30, F3

Kudos if you can locate this chic herbivore haven right away. Hint: it's upstairs past a giant chandelier in the service alley of the Westin Grand Hotel. Ring the bell to enter an elegantly industrial loft for flesh-free, flavour-packed dishes from current-harvest ingredients. (030-2749 2940; www.cookiescream.com; Behrenstrasse 55; mains €22, 3-course menu €39; from 7pm Tue-Sat; ; S Französische Strasse)

Ishin – Mittelstrasse JAPANESE €€

11 Map p30, F3

Look beyond the cafeteria-style get-up to sushi glory for minimal prices. Combination platters are ample and affordable, especially during happy hour (all day Wednesday and Saturday, until 4pm on other days). If you're not in the mood for raw fish, tuck into a steaming rice bowl topped with meat and/or veg. Nice touch: the unlimited free green tea. (www.ishin.de; Mittelstrasse 24; sushi platters €8-19.50, bowls €5-13; 11am-10pm Mon-Sat; S Friedrichstrasse, Friedrichstrasse)

Borchardt FRENCH €€€

12  Map p30, F4

Jagger, Clooney and Redford are among the celebs who have tucked into dry-aged steaks and plump oysters in the marble-pillared dining hall of this Berlin institution, established in 1853 by a caterer to the Kaiser. No dish, however, moves as fast as the Wiener Schnitzel, a wafer-thin slice of breaded veal fried to crisp perfection. (030-8188 6262; Französische Strasse 47; 3-course business lunch €15, dinner mains €20-40; 11.30am-1am; S Französische Strasse)

Augustiner am Gendarmenmarkt GERMAN €€

13  Map p30, G4

Tourists, concert-goers and hearty-food lovers rub shoulders at rustic tables in this surprisingly authentic Bavarian beer hall. Soak up the down-to-earth vibe right along with a mug of full-bodied Augustiner brew. Sausages, roast pork and pretzels provide rib-sticking sustenance, but there's also plenty of lighter (even meat-free) fare as well as good-value lunch specials. (030-2045 4020; www.augustiner-braeu-berlin.de; Charlottenstrasse 55; mains €6-19; 10am-2am; S Französische Strasse)

Soya Cosplay ASIAN €€

14  Map p30, G4

At this stylish contender, colourful lanterns and nifty lamps create cosiness without kitsch, and dishes on the menu are veritable aroma explosions. The pork belly beautifully plays off pungent Asian herbs, shrimp balls are perked up with wasabi mayonnaise, and even the jellyfish carpaccio is delicate rather than slimy. (030-2062

Haus der Kulturen der Welt (p35)

9093; www.soyacosplay.com; Jägerstrasse 59-60; plates €6-22; noon-midnight Mon-Sat, 5pm-midnight Sun; S Französische Strasse)

Chipps
VEGETARIAN €€

15 Map p30, H4

Well worth a little detour, this crisp corner spot with show kitchen and panorama windows turns heads with yummy cooked breakfasts (served all day on Sundays), build-your-own salads and creative hot specials that spin regional, seasonal ingredients into taste-bud magic. Most dishes are vegetarian, some are vegan. (030-3644 4588; www.chipps.eu; Jägerstrasse 35; mains €11-17; 9am-11pm Mon-Sat, 9am-5pm Sun; ; S Hausvogteiplatz)

Drinking

Tausend
BAR

16 Map p30, E2

No sign, no light, no bell, just an anonymous steel door tucked under a railway bridge leads to one of Berlin's chicest bars. Behind it, flirty frocks sip raspberry mojitos alongside London Mule–cradling three-day stubbles. The eye-catching decor channels '80s glam while DJs and bands fuel the vibe. (www.tausendberlin.com; Schiffbauerdamm 11; from 7.30pm Tue-Sat; S Friedrichstrasse, Friedrichstrasse)

Berliner Republik

PUB

17  Map p30, F2

Just as in a mini-stock exchange, the cost of drinks fluctuates with demand at this raucous riverside pub. Everyone goes Pavlovian when a heavy brass bell rings, signalling rock-bottom prices. You won't be hoisting mugs with many Berliners here, but it's a fun spot nonetheless. (030-3087 2293; www.die-berliner-republik.de; Schiffbauerdamm 8; 10am-6am; S Friedrichstrasse, Friedrichstrasse)

Bebel Bar

BAR

18 Map p30, G3

Plush luxury is the mojo of the Bebel Bar at the Hotel Rome, where the *Mad Men* crew would fit right in. Try a Roccos Mule, a heady mix of brandy, plum, fresh raspberries, lemon and spicy ginger. On balmy nights, the action moves to the rooftop terrace. (030-460 6090; www.hotelderome.com; Behrenstrasse 37; 9am-1am; 100, 200, TXL, S Hausvogteiplatz)

Felix

CLUB

19  Map p30, D4

Once past the velvet rope of this swanky club, you too can shake your booty to high-octane hip-hop, dance and disco beats, sip Champagne cocktails, watch the crowd from the gallery and flirt up a storm. Women get free entry and a glass of Prosecco until midnight on Mondays, while the worker-bee brigade kicks loose on after-work Thursdays. (030-301 117 152; www.felix-clubrestaurant.de; Behrenstrasse 72; from 11pm Mon, Fri & Sat, from 7pm Thu; S Brandenburger Tor, Brandenburger Tor)

Entertainment

Konzerthaus Berlin

CLASSICAL MUSIC

20 Map p30, G4

This top-ranked concert hall – a Schinkel design from 1821 – counts the Konzerthaus-Orchester as its 'house band' but also hosts international soloists, thematic concert cycles, children's events and concerts by the Rundfunk-Sinfonieorchester Berlin. Guided tours (€3, in German) at 1pm on Saturdays. (tickets 030-203 092 101; www.konzerthaus.de; Gendarmenmarkt 2; S Stadtmitte, Französische Strasse)

Admiralspalast

PERFORMING ARTS

21 Map p30, F2

This beautifully restored 1920s 'palace' stages crowd-pleasing plays, concerts and comedy shows in its glamorous historic main hall. More intimate programs are presented on the smaller studio stage on the 4th floor. Most performances are suitable for non-German speakers, but do check ahead. (tickets 030-2250 7000; www.admiralspalast.de; Friedrichstrasse 101; S Friedrichstrasse, Friedrichstrasse)

Tipi am Kanzleramt

CABARET

22  Map p30, A2

Tipi stages a year-round program of high-calibre cabaret, dance, acrobatics, musical comedy and magic shows starring German and international artists. It's all staged in a huge and festively decorated permanent tent stationed between the Federal Chancellery and the House of World Cultures on the edge of Tiergarten park. Pre-show dinner is available. (☎tickets 030-3906 6550; www.tipi-am-kanzleramt.de; Grosse Querallee; 🚌100, S Bundestag, 🚆Hauptbahnhof)

Shopping

Dussmann – Das Kulturkaufhaus BOOKS, MUSIC

23  Map p30, F3

It's easy to lose track of time in this cultural playground with wall-to-wall books, DVDs and CDs, leaving no genre unaccounted for. Bonus points for the free reading-glass rentals, downstairs cafe and performance space used for concerts, political discussions and high-profile book readings and signings. (☎030-2025 1111; www.kulturkaufhaus.de; Friedrichstrasse 90; ⏲9am-midnight Mon-Fri, to 11.30pm Sat; S Friedrichstrasse, 🚆Friedrichstrasse)

Fassbender & Rausch FOOD

24  Map p30, G5

If the Aztecs thought of chocolate as the elixir of the gods, then this emporium of truffles and pralines must be heaven. Bonus: the chocolate volcano and giant replicas of Berlin landmarks. The upstairs cafe-restaurant has views of Gendarmenmarkt and serves sinful drinking chocolates and cakes as well as dishes prepared and seasoned with cocoa. (☎030-2045 8443; www.fassbender-rausch.com; Charlottenstrasse 60; ⏲10am-8pm Mon-Sat, 11am-8pm Sun; S Stadtmitte)

Galeries Lafayette DEPARTMENT STORE

25 Map p30, F4

Stop by the Berlin branch of the exquisite French fashion emporium if only to check out the show-stealing interior (designed by Jean Nouvel, no less), centred on a huge glass cone shimmering with kaleidoscopic intensity. Around it wrap three circular floors filled with fancy fashions, fragrances and accessories, while glorious gourmet treats await downstairs in the food hall. (☎030-209 480; www.galeries lafayette.de; Friedrichstrasse 76-78; ⏲10am-8pm Mon-Sat; S Französische Strasse)

Top Tip

Free Concerts

The gifted students at Berlin's top-rated classical music academy, the **Hochschule für Musik Hanns Eisler** (Map p30, G4; ☎tickets 030-203 092 101; www.hfm-berlin.de; Charlottenstrasse 55; S Stadtmitte, Französische Strasse), showcase their talents in several recitals weekly, most of them for free or low-cost. They're held either on the main campus or nearby in the Neuer Marstall at Schlossplatz 7.

Explore

Museum Island & Alexanderplatz

Walk through ancient Babylon, meet an Egyptian queen, clamber up a Greek altar or study Monet's moody landscapes. There are treasures galore on Museum Island, a Unesco-recognised cluster of five repositories brimming with art and architecture from Europe and beyond. Berlin's medieval birthplace, Nikolaiviertel, is nearby, serenaded by the spiky TV Tower anchoring noisy, socialist-flavoured Alexanderplatz.

The Sights in a Day

Avoid queuing for the **Pergamonmuseum** (p42) by buying an early timeslot ticket online, then devote at least a couple of hours to marvelling at its ancient treasures – the Ishtar Gate, the Market Gate of Miletus etc. Snap a picture of the **Berliner Dom** (p49) then head over to the **Humboldt-Box** (p145) to find out what the fuss is all about with the reconstruction of the Berlin City Palace and to enjoy a leisurely lunch with a view from the rooftop cafe.

Energy restored, pay your respects to Queen Nefertiti at the **Neues Museum** (p46) or match your interests to any of the other Museum Island contenders. Afterwards, process your impressions during a leisurely **river cruise** (p52) through Berlin's historic centre, then finish up with a late-afternoon bird's-eye view of the city from the top of the **TV Tower** (p49), Germany's tallest structure.

If you want an old-timey dinner experience, wrap up the day with a traditional German meal at **Zur Letzten Instanz** (p51), or head to **Zwölf Apostel** (p52) for wagon-wheel-size pizza.

Top Sights

Pergamonmuseum (p42)

Neues Museum (p46)

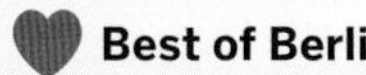

Best of Berlin

Museums

Altes Museum (p49)

Neues Museum (p46)

Pergamonmuseum (p42)

DDR Museum (p49)

Eating

Zur Letzten Instanz (p51)

Getting There

Bus The 100, 200 and TXL link Alexanderplatz with Museum Island.

S S-Bahn The S5, S7/75 and S9 all converge at Alexanderplatz. For Museum Island, Hackescher Markt and Friedrichstrasse stations are closer.

Tram The M1 and 12 stop at Am Kupfergraben west of Museum Island.

U U-Bahn The U2, U5 and U8 stop at Alexanderplatz. Friedrichstrasse is the closest station to Museum Island.

Top Sights Pergamonmuseum

Even when undergoing renovation, the Pergamonmuseum still opens a fascinating window onto the ancient world. The palatial three-wing complex unites a rich feast of classical sculpture and monumental architecture from Greece, Rome, Babylon and the Middle East in three collections: the Collection of Antiquities, the Museum of Near Eastern Antiquities and, upstairs, the Museum of Islamic Art. Most of it was excavated and spirited to Berlin by German archaeologists at the turn of the 20th century. Note that the namesake Pergamon Altar will be off limits until 2019.

Map p48, A2

030-266 424 242

www.smb.museum

Bodestrasse 1-3

adult/concession €12/6

10am-6pm Fri-Wed, to 8pm Thu

100, Hackescher Markt, Friedrichstrasse

Orpheus floor mosaic

Don't Miss

Market Gate of Miletus

Merchants and customers once flooded through this splendid 17m-high gate into the bustling market square of Miletus, a wealthy Roman trading town in today's Turkey. A strong earthquake levelled much of the town in the 11th century, but German archaeologists dug up the site between 1903 and 1905 and managed to put the puzzle back together. The richly decorated marble gate blends Greek and Roman design features and was probably built to welcome Emperor Hadrian on his AD 126 visit to Miletus.

Orpheus Floor Mosaic

Also from Miletus hails this beautifully restored floor mosaic starring Orpheus, a gifted musician from ancient Greek mythology whose lyre playing charmed even the beasts surrounding him. It originally graced the dining room of a 2nd-century Roman villa.

Ishtar Gate

Expect your jaw to drop as you face the magnificence of this reconstructed Babylonian town gate, Processional Way and facade of the throne hall of its builder, King Nebuchadnezzar II (604–562 BC). The walls of the gate are sheathed in radiant blue and ochre glazed bricks with friezes of strutting lions, bulls and dragons representing Babylonian gods. They're so striking you can almost imagine hearing the roaring and fanfare.

Clay Tablets from Uruk

Founded in the 4th millennium BC, Uruk (in present-day Iraq) is considered one of the world's first 'mega-cities', with as many as 40,000 inhabitants and more than 9km of city walls. Among the museum's most prized possessions are clay

Top Tips

- Skip the queue and save a little money by prepurchasing slightly discounted timeslot tickets online.
- Avoid the worst crowds by arriving early or late on weekdays.
- Pick up the excellent free audioguide.
- The Museumsinsel 'area ticket' (adult/concession €18/9) is valid for one-time, same-day admission to the permanent exhibits of the Pergamonmuseum, Altes Museum, Bodemuseum, Alte Nationalgalerie and Neues Museum.

Take a Break

During renovation, the nearest cafe is Allegretto (p47) at the adjacent Neues Museum (accessible without admission ticket).

A short walk away, Zwölf Apostel (p52) has lunchtime pizza specials.

tablets with cuneiform scripts detailing agreements and transactions that are considered the earliest written documents known to humankind.

Stela of Hammurabi

Back in the 18th century BC, King Hammurabi of Babylon decided to assert his royal authority by having his law decrees carved into an imposing stela (upright stone slab), a copy of which anchors the Babylonian Hall. Despite their ancient pedigree, some of the phrases are still heard today, including 'an eye for an eye; a tooth for a tooth'.

Statue of Hadad

Room 2, at the far end of the Museum of Near Eastern Antiquities, showcases treasures from ancient Assyria. It is lorded over by a monumental 2800-year-old statue of a fierce-looking Hadad, the West Semitic god of storm, thunder and rain. Also note the four lion sculptures guarding the partly reconstructed inner gate of the citadel of Samal (in today's Turkey).

Caliph's Palace of Mshatta

When Ottoman sultan Abdul Hamid II wanted to get into Emperor Wilhelm II's good graces, he gave him a most generous gift: the facade of the 8th-century palace of Mshatta, in today's Jordan. A masterpiece of early Islamic art, it depicts animals and mythical creatures frolicking peacefully amid a riot of floral motifs in an allusion

Pergamonmuseum

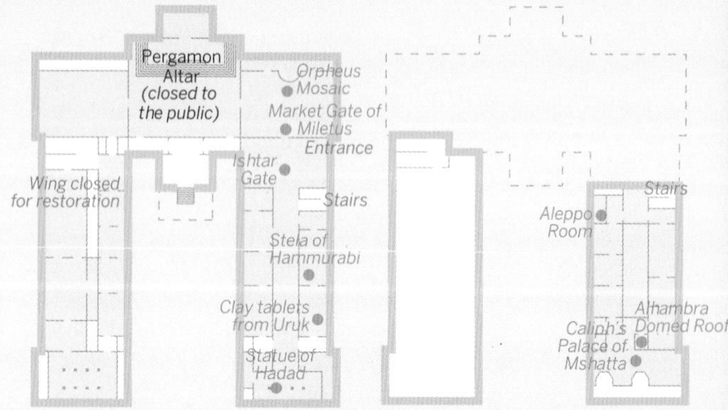

Understand

Museum Island Master Plan

The Pergamonmuseum is part of Museum Island (Museumsinsel), a cluster of museums that collectively became a Unesco World Heritage Site in 1999. The distinction was at least partly achieved because of a master plan for the renovation and modernisation of the complex, which is expected to be completed in 2025 under the aegis of British architect David Chipperfield. Except for the Pergamon – now under renovation – the restoration of the buildings themselves has been completed. Construction has also begun on the James-Simon-Galerie, a colonnaded modern foyer that will serve as the central entrance to four of the five museums and also harbour a cafe and other service facilities. Another key feature of the master plan is the 'Archaeological Promenade' that will eventually link the four archaeological museums underground. For details see www.museumsinsel-berlin.de.

to the Garden of Eden. It's upstairs in Room 9 in the Islamic Museum.

Alhambra Domed Roof

A domed cedar and poplar ceiling from the Torre de las Damas (Ladies' Tower) of the Alhambra in southern Spain's Granada forms the 'lid of the Moorish Cabinet' in the Islamic Museum. Intricately patterned, it centres on a 16-pointed star from which radiate 16 triangular panels inlaid with decorative elements.

Aleppo Room

Guests arriving in this richly painted, wood-panelled reception room would have had no doubt of the wealth and power of its owner, a Christian merchant in 17th-century Aleppo, Syria. The beautiful, if dizzying, decorations combine Islamic floral and geometric motifs with courtly scenes and Christian themes. Look closely to make out *The Last Supper* to the right of the central door.

Top Sights
Neues Museum

David Chipperfield's reconstruction of the bombed-out New Museum on Museum Island is the new home of the show-stopping Egyptian Museum (headlined by Queen Nefertiti) and the equally enthralling Museum of Pre- and Early History. Like he was completing a giant jigsaw puzzle, the British star architect incorporated every original shard, scrap and brick he could find into the new structure. This brilliant blend of the historic and the modern creates a dynamic space that beautifully juxtaposes massive stairwells, domed rooms, muralled halls and high ceilings.

Map p48, B3

030-266 424 242

www.smb.museum

Bodestrasse 1-3

adult/concession €12/6

10am-6pm Fri-Wed, 10am-8pm Thu

100, 200, Hackescher Markt

Egyptian sarcophagi

Don't Miss

Nefertiti

An audience with Berlin's most beautiful woman, the 3330-year-old Queen Nefertiti – she of the long graceful neck and timeless good looks – is a must. The bust was part of the treasure trove unearthed by a Berlin expedition of archaeologists around 1912 while sifting through the sands of Armana, the royal city built by Nefertiti's husband, King Akhenaten.

Berliner Goldhut

Resembling a wizard's hat, the 3000-year-old Berlin Gold Hat must indeed have struck the Bronze Age people as something magical. The entire cone is swathed in elaborate bands of astrological symbols believed to have helped priests calculate the movements of sun and moon and thus predict the best times for planting and harvesting. It's one of only four unearthed worldwide.

Berlin Grüner Kopf

A key item from the Late Egyptian Period, which shows Greek influence, is the so-called Berlin 'Green Head' (c 400 BC), the bald head of a priest carved from smooth green stone. Unusually for art from this period, the sculptor did not create a realistic portrait of a specific person but rather sought to convey universal wisdom and experience.

Trojan Collection

Three humble-looking silver jars are the star exhibits among the Trojan antiquities discovered by archaeologist Heinrich Schliemann in 1870 near Hisarlik in today's Turkey. Many other objects on display, including elaborate jewellery, ornate weapons and gold mugs, are replicas because the originals were looted by the Soviets after WWII and remain in Moscow to this day.

☑ Top Tips

- Skip the queue and save a bit by buying timeslot tickets online in advance. The museum may only be entered during your designated half-hour timeslot but you're free to stay as long as you wish.
- Tours (in German, €4) focusing on the museum's history and highlights take place at 11.30am Sunday. No prebooking is required.
- The Museumsinsel 'area ticket' (adult/concession €18/9) is valid for one-time, same-day admission to the Neues Museum, Altes Museum, Bodemuseum, Alte Nationalgalerie and Pergamonmuseum.

Take a Break

The lure of potent java and homemade snacks keeps the on-site **Allegretto** (dishes €2-9) cafe abuzz.

A
B
C
D
E
1
2
3
4
Oranienburger Str
Krausnickstr
Grosse Hamburger
Sophienstr
SCHEUNENVIERTEL
Weinmeisterstr
Schönhauser Str
Münzstr
Max-Beer-Str
Almstadtstr
Hirtenstr
Prenzlauer Allee
Wadzeck Str
Keibelstr
Oranienburger Str
Memhardstr
Am Alexanderplatz
Ziegelstr
Monbijoustr
Monbijouplatz
Monbijou Park
Hackescher Markt
Dircksenstr
Alexanderplatz
Otto-Braun-
Hackescher Markt
Rochstr
Bodemuseum
Pergamonmuseum
Spree River
Burgstr
Anna-Karsch-Str
Rosenstr
Karl-Liebknecht-Str
Alexanderplatz
Alexanderplatz
Karl-Marx-Allee
Am Kupfergraben
Georgenstr
Alte Nationalgalerie
Friedrichbrücke
Fernsehturm
Berlin Tourismus
Jacobystr
Bauhofstr
Neues Museum
Bodestr
Am Lustgarten
Berliner Dom
DDR Museum
Altes Museum
Alexanderstr
Am Zeughaus
Lustgarten
Karl-Liebknecht-Str
Liebknechtbrücke
Jüdenstr
Grunerstr
Littenstr
Unter den Linden
Schlossbrücke
MUSEUM ISLAND (MUSEUMSINSEL)
Spandauer Str
Klosterstr
Voltairestr
Nikolaiviertel
Spreekanal
Schlossplatz
Rathausstr
Waisenstr
Molkenmarkt
Werderscher Markt
Breite Str
Stralauer Str
Schicklerstr
Jannowitzbrücke
0
200 m
1
2
3
4
5
6
7
8
9
10
11
12
13
14
15
16
17
For reviews see
Top Sights p42
Sights p49
Eating p51
Drinking p52

Sights

DDR Museum

MUSEUM

1 Map p48, B3

This interactive museum does a delightful job at pulling back the iron curtain on an extinct society. Find out that East German kids were put through collective potty training, engineers earned little more than farmers and everyone, it seems, went on nudist holidays. A highlight is a simulated ride in a Trabi. (GDR Museum; 030-847 123 731; www.ddr-museum.de; Karl-Liebknecht-Strasse 1; adult/concession €6/4; 10am-8pm Sun-Fri, 10am-10pm Sat; ; 100, 200, Hackescher Markt)

Altes Museum

MUSEUM

2 Map p48, B3

A curtain of fluted columns gives way to the Pantheon-inspired rotunda of the grand neoclassical Old Museum, which harbours a prized antiquities collection. In the downstairs galleries, sculptures, vases, tomb reliefs and jewellery shed light on various facets of life in ancient Greece, while upstairs the focus is on the Etruscans and Romans. Top draws include the *Praying Boy* bronze sculpture, Roman silver vessels, an 'erotic cabinet' (over 18s only!) and portraits of Caesar and Cleopatra. (Old Museum; 030-266 424 242; www.smb.museum; Am Lustgarten; adult/concession €10/5; 10am-6pm Tue, Wed & Fri-Sun, 10am-8pm Thu; 100, 200, Friedrichstrasse, Hackescher Markt)

Berliner Dom

CHURCH

3 Map p48, B3

Pompous yet majestic, the Italian Renaissance-style former royal court church (1905) does triple duty as house of worship, museum and concert hall. Inside it's gilt to the hilt and outfitted with a lavish marble-and-onyx altar, a 7269-pipe Sauer organ and elaborate royal sarcophagi. Climb up the 267 steps to the gallery for glorious city views. (Berlin Cathedral; 030-2026 9136; www.berlinerdom.de; Am Lustgarten; adult/concession/under 18yr €7/4/free; 9am-8pm Mon-Sat, noon-8pm Sun, Apr-Sep, to 7pm Oct-Mar; 100, 200, Hackescher Markt)

Fernsehturm

LANDMARK

4 Map p48, D2

Germany's tallest structure, the 368m-high TV Tower is as iconic to Berlin as the Eiffel Tower is to Paris. On clear days, views from the panorama level at 203m are unbeatable. The upstairs Restaurant Sphere (mains €14 to 28) makes one revolution per hour. To skip the line, buy tickets online. (030-247 575 875; www.tv-turm.de; Panoramastrasse 1a; adult/child €13/8.50, Fast View ticket €19.50/11.50; 9am-midnight Mar-Oct, 10am-midnight Nov-Feb; S Alexanderplatz, Alexanderplatz)

Bodemuseum

MUSEUM

5 Map p48, A2

On the northern tip of Museum Island, this palatial edifice by Ernst von Ihne houses European sculpture from the Middle Ages to the 18th

Understand

Red Berlin: Life in the GDR

Two Germanys

The formal division of Germany in 1949 resulted in the western zones becoming the Bundesrepublik Deutschland (BRD; Federal Republic of Germany, FRG) with Bonn as its capital, and the Soviet zone morphing into the Deutsche Demokratische Republik (DDR; German Democratic Republic, GDR) with East Berlin as its capital. Despite the latter's name, only one party – the Sozialistische Einheitspartei Deutschlands (SED; Socialist Unity Party of Germany) – controlled all policy until 1989.

The Stasi

In order to oppress any opposition, the GDR government established the Ministry for State Security (Stasi) in 1950 and put millions of its own citizens under surveillance. Tactics included wire-tapping, videotape observation and the opening of private mail. Real or suspected regime critics often ended up in Stasi-run prisons. The organisation grew steadily in power and size, and by the end had 91,000 official full-time employees plus 173,000 informants. The latter were recruited among regular folk to spy on their co-workers, friends, family and neighbours as well as on people in West Germany.

Economic Woes & the Wall

While West Germany blossomed in the 1950s, thanks to the US-sponsored Marshall Plan economic aid package, East Germany stagnated, partly because of the Soviets' continued policy of asset stripping and reparation payments. As the economic gulf widened, scores of mostly young and educated East Germans decided to seek a future in the west, further straining the economy and leading to the construction of the Berlin Wall in 1961 to stop the exodus.

The appointment of Erich Honecker in 1971 opened the way for rapprochement with the west. Honecker fell in line with Soviet politics but his economic approach did improve the East German economy, eventually leading to the collapse of the regime and the fall of the Berlin Wall in November 1989.

century, including key works by Tilmann Riemenschneider, Donatello and Giovanni Pisano. Other rooms harbour a huge coin collection and Byzantine art from elaborate sarcophagi to ivory carvings and mosaic icons. (030-266 424 242; www.smb.museum; Am Kupfergraben/Monbijoubrücke; adult/concession €10/5; 10am-6pm Tue, Wed & Fri-Sun, 10am-8pm Thu; Hackescher Markt)

Alte Nationalgalerie MUSEUM

6 Map p48, B2

The Greek-temple-style Old National Gallery is a three-storey showcase of 19th-century European art. To get a sense of the period's virtuosity, pay special attention to Franz Krüger and Adolf Menzel's canvases glorifying Prussia and to the moody landscapes by Romantic heart-throb Caspar David Friedrich. There's also a sprinkling of French impressionists in case you're keen on seeing yet another version of Monet's *Water Lilies*. (Old National Gallery; 030-266 424 242; www.smb.museum; Bodestrasse 1-3; adult/concession €10/5; 10am-6pm Tue, Wed & Fri-Sun, 10am-8pm Thu; 100, 200, Hackescher Markt)

Eating

Brauhaus Georgbräu GERMAN €€

7 Map p48, C4

Tourist-geared but cosy, this brewpub is the only place where you can guzzle the local St Georg pilsner. In winter the woodsy beer hall is perfect for tucking into hearty Berlin-style goulash or *Eisbein* (boiled pork knuckle), while in summer the riverside beer garden beckons. (030-242 4244; www.georgbraeu.de; Spreeufer 4; mains €10-14; 12pm-midnight; S Klosterstrasse)

Dolores CALIFORNIAN €

8 Map p48, D1

Dolores is a bastion of California-style burritos – fresh, authentic and priced to help you stay on budget. The 'Calimex' menu is organised module-style with you selecting your favourite combo of marinated meats (the lime coriander chicken is yummy) or tofu, rice, beans, veggies, cheese and salsa, and the cheerful staff will build it on the spot. There's even a tortilla-less 'burrito-in-a-bowl' for carbophobes. Great homemade lemonade, too. (030-2809 9597; www.dolores-online.de; Rosa-Luxemburg-Strasse 7; burritos €4-6; 11.30am-10pm Mon-Sat, 1-10pm Sun; 100, 200, S Alexanderplatz, Alexanderplatz)

Zur Letzten Instanz GERMAN €€

9  Map p48, E4

Oozing folksy Old Berlin charm, this rustic eatery has been an enduring hit since 1621 and has fed everyone from Napoleon to Beethoven to Angela Merkel. Although now tourist-geared, the food quality is still pretty high when it comes to such local rib-stickers as *Grillhaxe* (grilled pork knuckle) and *Bouletten* (meat patties). (030-242 5528; www.zurletzteninstanz.de; Waisenstrasse 14-16; mains €9-18; noon-1am Mon-Sat, noon-11pm Sun; S Klosterstrasse)

Top Tip

Sightseeing River Cruises

A lovely way to experience Berlin from April to October is from the open-air deck of a river cruiser. Several companies run relaxing one-hour (about €9) Spree spins through the city centre from landing docks just north of Museum Island. Sip refreshments while a guide showers you with tidbits as you glide past grand old buildings, beach bars and the government quarter.

Hofbräuhaus Berlin — GERMAN €€

10 Map p48, E1

Popular with coach tourists and field-tripping teens, this giant beer hall with 2km of wooden benches serves the same litre-size mugs of beer and big plates of German fare as the Munich original. A brass band and dirndl- and lederhosen-clad servers add further faux authenticity. (030-679 665 520; www.hofbraeuhaus-berlin.de; Karl-Liebknecht-Strasse 30; mains €4-18; 10am-1am Sun-Thu, 10am-2am Fri & Sat; 100, 200, S Alexanderplatz, Alexanderplatz)

Zwölf Apostel — ITALIAN €€

11 Map p48, A2

A pleasant pit stop between museums, this place beneath the railway arches has over-the-top religious decor and tasty thin-crust pizzas named after the 12 apostles. (www.12-apostel.de; Georgenstrasse 2; mains €8-16; M1, S Friedrichstrasse, Friedrichstrasse)

Drinking

Strandbar Mitte — BAR

12 Map p48, A2

With a full-on view of the Bodemuseum, palm trees and a relaxed ambience, Germany's first beach bar (since 2002) is great for balancing a surfeit of sightseeing stimulus with a revivifying drink. At night, there's dancing under the stars with tango, cha cha, swing and salsa. (030-2838 5588; www.strandbar-mitte.de; Monbijoustrasse 3; 10am-late May-Sep; M1, Oranienburger Strasse)

House of Weekend — CLUB

13 Map p48, E2

After a facelift, the former Weekend reopened in summer 2014 with the same sophisticated summertime rooftop terrace for cocktails and barbecue with stunning views. After 11pm, the cadre of shiny happy people moves down to the studio (15th) floor for sweet dance sounds, mostly electro from local DJs, with the occasional excursion into hip hop and dubstep. (reservations 0152 2429 3140; www.houseofweekend.berlin; Am Alexanderplatz 5; roof garden from 7pm weather permitting, studio floor from 11pm; S Alexanderplatz, Alexanderplatz)

Club Avenue @ Café Moskau — CLUB

14 Map p48, E2

This high-octane club has taken over the cellar of Café Moskau, a protected East Berlin landmark. Dress to impress the doormen in order to gyrate on the dance floor to hip hop, house and disco. The retro interior is the work of the decorating team behind Berghain/Panoramabar. It's also the new home of the **GMF** (030-2809 5396; www.gmf-berlin.de; 11pm Sun) gay Sunday party. (0174 600 3000; www.avenue-berlin.com; Karl-Marx-Allee 34; from 10pm Thu, from 11pm Fri & Sat; S Schillingstrasse)

Shopping

ausberlin GIFTS, SOUVENIRS

15 Map p48, D2

'Made in Berlin' is the motto of this hip store where you can source the latest BPitch or Ostgut CD, eccentric ubo jewellery, wittily printed linen bags and all sorts of other knick-knacks (anti-monster spray anyone?) designed right here in this fair city. (030-4199 7896; www.ausberlin.de; Karl-Liebknecht-Strasse 17; 10am-8pm Mon-Sat; 100, 200, S Alexanderplatz, Alexanderplatz)

Galeria Kaufhof DEPARTMENT STORE

16 Map p48, D2

A total renovation by the late John P Kleihues turned this former GDR-era department store into a retail cube fit for the 21st century, complete with a glass-domed light court and a sleek travertine skin that glows green at night. There's little you won't find on the five football-field-size floors, including a gourmet supermarket on the ground floor. (030-247 430; www.galeria-kaufhof.de; Alexanderplatz 9; 9.30am-8pm Mon-Wed, to 10pm Thu-Sat; S Alexanderplatz, Alexanderplatz)

Alexa SHOPPING MALL

17 Map p48, E3

José Quintela da Fonseca designed this XXL mall that power-shoppers love. The predictable range of high-street retailers is here, plus a few more upmarket stores like Swarovski, Crumpler, Adidas Neo and Triumph. Good food court for a bite on the run. (030-269 3400; www.alexacentre.com; Grunerstrasse 20; 10am-9pm Mon-Sat; S Alexanderplatz, Alexanderplatz)

JOHN FREEMAN/GETTY IMAGES ©

Alexa shopping mall

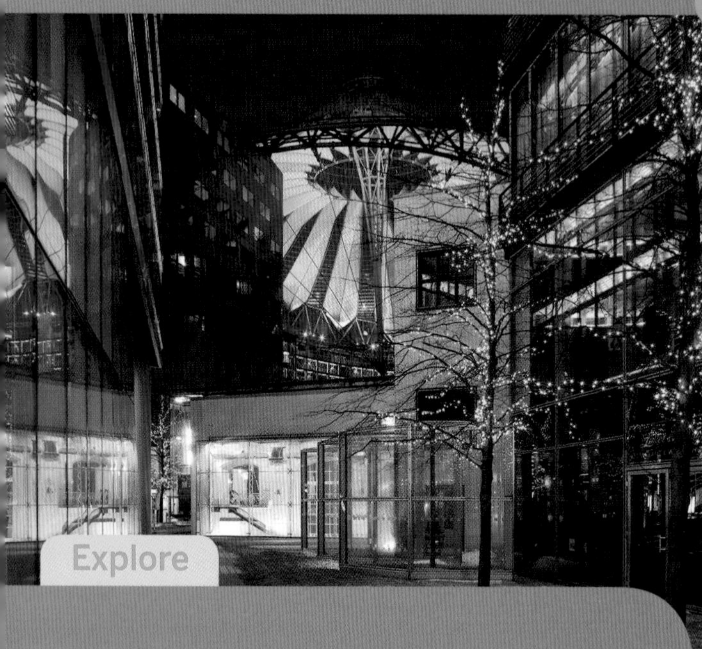

Explore

Potsdamer Platz

Despite the name, Potsdamer Platz is not just a square but Berlin's newest quarter, birthed in the '90s from terrain once bisected by the Berlin Wall. A collaborative effort by the world's finest architects, it is a vibrant showcase of urban renewal. A visit here is easily combined with the Kulturforum, a cluster of top-notch museums and concert halls, including the world-famous Berliner Philharmonie.

The Sights in a Day

Start the day getting the lay of the land by whizzing to the top of the **Panoramapunkt** (p61) for bird's-eye views of Berlin's landmarks, perhaps over a coffee. Make your way to the **Gemäldegalerie** (p56) for a rendezvous with Rembrandt and Co then once you've exhausted your attention span head back to Potsdamer Platz and join the business brigade for lunch at **Qiu** (p68).

It's time to take a closer look at the futuristic architecture of the **Sony Center** (p61) before spending the afternoon delving first into the darkness of the Nazi era at the **Topographie des Terrors** (p65) and then the Cold War at **Checkpoint Charlie** (p65). By now you're probably ready for a drink, so head to **Solar** (p69) for libations with a view.

Either have an early meal at **Vapiano** (p68) before catching a concert at the **Berliner Philharmonie** (p69) or treat yourself to an evening of Michelin-starred cuisine at **Restaurant Tim Raue** (p68).

Top Sights

Gemäldegalerie (p56)

Potsdamer Platz (p60)

Jüdisches Museum (p62)

Best of Berlin

Historical Sites

Topographie des Terrors (p65)

Gedenkstätte Deutscher Widerstand (p66)

Checkpoint Charlie (p65)

Art

Gemäldegalerie (p56)

Museums

Museum für Film und Fernsehen (p61)

Music & Performance

Berliner Philharmonie (p69)

Getting There

Bus The 200 comes from Zoologischer Garten and Alexanderplatz, the M41 from the Hauptbahnhof and the M29 from Checkpoint Charlie.

S-Bahn The S1, S2 and S25 stop at Potsdamer Platz.

U-Bahn Handy stops on the U2 include Potsdamer Platz and Mendelssohn-Bartholdy-Park. The U6 stops near Checkpoint Charlie (Kochstrasse).

Top Sights
Gemäldegalerie

When the Picture Gallery, Berlin's grand survey of Old Masters, opened in its custom-built Kulturforum space in 1998, it marked the happy reunion of an outstanding collection of European paintings separated by the Cold War for half a century. About 1500 works span the arc of artistic vision between the 13th and 18th centuries. Rooms radiating from the football-field-size central foyer brim with key canvases by Rembrandt, Titian, Goya, Botticelli, Holbein, Gainsborough, Canaletto, Hals, Rubens, Vermeer and other heavy hitters.

Map p64, A2

www.smb.museum/gg

Matthäikirchplatz 8

adult/concession €10/5

10am-6pm Tue, Wed & Fri-Sun, 10am-8pm Thu

M29, M41, 200, S Potsdamer Platz, Potsdamer Platz

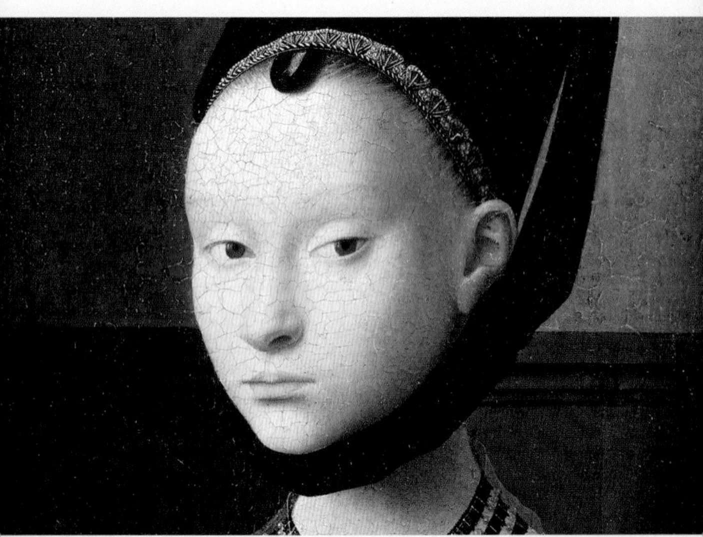

Portrait of a Young Lady (p59)

Don't Miss

Amor Victorius (1602–03)

Room XIV

That's quite a cheeky fellow peering down on viewers, isn't it? Wearing nothing but a mischievous grin and a pair of black angel wings, with a fistful of arrows, this Amor means business. In this famous painting, Caravaggio shows off his amazing talent at depicting objects with near-photographic realism achieved by his ingeniously theatrical use of light and shadow.

Dutch Proverbs (1559)

Room 7

In this moralistic yet humorous painting, Dutch Renaissance painter Pieter Bruegel the Elder manages to illustrate more than 100 proverbs and idioms in a single seaside village scene. While some emphasise the absurdity of human behaviour, others unmask its imprudence and sinfulness. Some sayings are still in use today, among them 'swimming against the tide' and 'armed to the teeth'.

Portrait of Hieronymus Holzschuher (1526)

Room 2

Hieronymus Holzschuher was a Nuremberg patrician, a career politician and a strong supporter of the Reformation. He was also a friend of one of the greatest German Renaissance painters, Albrecht Dürer. In this portrait, which shows its sitter at age 57, the artist brilliantly lasers in on Holzschuher's features with utmost precision, down to the furrows, wrinkles and thinning hair.

Woman with a Pearl Necklace (1662–64)

Room 18

No, it's not the *Girl with a Pearl Earring* of book and movie fame, but it's still one of Jan Vermeer's

☑ Top Tips

- Take advantage of the excellent free audioguide to get the low-down on selected works.
- A tour of all 72 rooms covers almost 2km, so allow at least a couple of hours for your visit and wear comfortable shoes.
- Admission is free to anyone under 18.
- A ticket to the Gemäldegalerie also gets you same-day admission to the permanent collections of the other Kulturforum museums.

Take a Break

The upstairs cafeteria has a salad bar, precooked meals (around €6) and hot and cold beverages.

Good lunch spots on nearby Potsdamer Platz are Vapiano (p68), Qiu (p68) and the food court in the Potsdamer Platz Arkaden.

most famous paintings: a young woman studies herself in the mirror while fastening a pearl necklace. A top dog among Dutch Realist painters, Vermeer mesmerises viewers by beautifully capturing this intimate moment with characteristic soft brushstrokes.

Fountain of Youth (1546)

Room III

Lucas Cranach the Elder's poignant painting illustrates humankind's yearning for eternal youth. Old crones plunge into a pool of water and emerge as dashing hotties – this fountain would surely put plastic surgeons out of business. The transition is reflected in the landscape, which is stark and craggy on the left, and lush and fertile on the right.

Malle Babbe (1633)

Room 13

Frans Hals ingeniously captures the character and vitality of his subject, 'Crazy Barbara', with free-wielding brushstrokes. Hals met the woman with the almost demonic laugh in the workhouse for the mentally ill where his son Pieter was also a resident. The tin mug and owl are symbols of Babbe's fondness for tipple.

Leda with the Swan (1532)

Room XVI

Judging by her blissed-out expression, Leda is having a fine time with that swan who, according to Greek mythology, is none other than Zeus himself. The erotically charged nature of this painting by Italian Renaissance artist

Gemäldegalerie

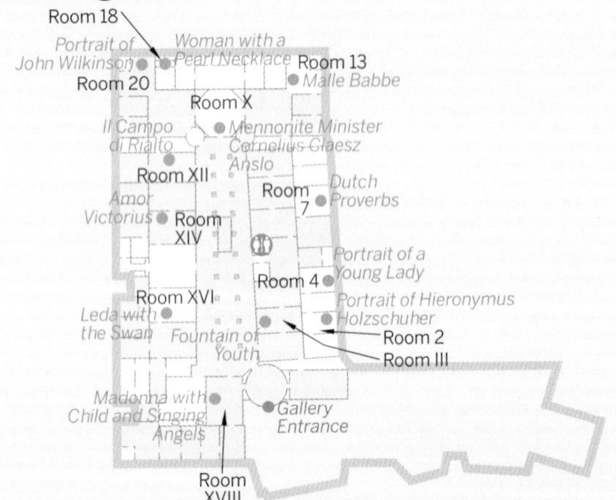

Correggio apparently so incensed its one-time owner Louis of Orleans that he cut off Leda's head with a knife. It was later restored.

Portrait of a Young Lady (1470)

Room 4

Berlin's own 'Mona Lisa' may not be as famous as the real thing but she's quite intriguing nonetheless. Who is this woman with the almond-shaped eyes and porcelain skin who gazes straight at us with a blend of sadness and skepticism? This famous portrait is a key work by Petrus Christus and his only one depicting a woman.

Madonna with Child and Singing Angels (1477)

Room XVIII

Renaissance artist Sandro Botticelli's circular painting (a format called a *tondo*) is a symmetrical composition showing Mary at the centre flanked by two sets of four wingless angels. It's an intimate moment that shows the Virgin tenderly embracing – perhaps even about to breastfeed – her child. The white lilies are symbols of her purity.

Mennonite Minister Cornelius Claesz Anslo (1641)

Room X

A masterpiece in the gallery's prized Rembrandt collection, this large-scale canvas shows the cloth merchant and Mennonite preacher Anslo in conversation with his wife. The huge open Bible and his gesturing hand sticking out in almost 3D style from the centre of the painting are meant to emphasise the strength of his religious convictions.

Portrait of John Wilkinson (1775)

Room 20

Works by Thomas Gainsborough are rarely seen outside the UK, which is what makes this portrait of British industrialist John Wilkinson so special. Nicknamed 'Iron Mad Wilkinson' for pioneering the making and use of cast iron, here he is – somewhat ironically – shown in a natural setting, almost blending in with his surroundings.

Il Campo di Rialto (1758–63)

Room XII

Giovanni Antonio Canal, aka Canaletto, studied painting in the workshop of his theatre-set-designer father. Here he depicts the Campo di Rialto, the arcaded main market square of his hometown, Venice, with stunning precision and perspective. Note the goldsmith shops on the left, the wig-wearing merchants in the centre and the stores selling paintings and furniture on the right.

Top Sights
Potsdamer Platz

Potsdamer Platz 2.0 is essentially a modern reinterpretation of the historic original, which was the equivalent of New York's Times Square until WWII sucked all life out of the area. It's divided into three slices: DaimlerCity, with a large mall, public art and high-profile entertainment venues; the flashy Sony Center, built around a central plaza canopied by a glass roof that shimmers in myriad colours at night; and the comparatively subdued Beisheim Center, which was inspired by classic US skyscraper design.

Map p64, C2

200, S Potsdamer Platz, Potsdamer Platz

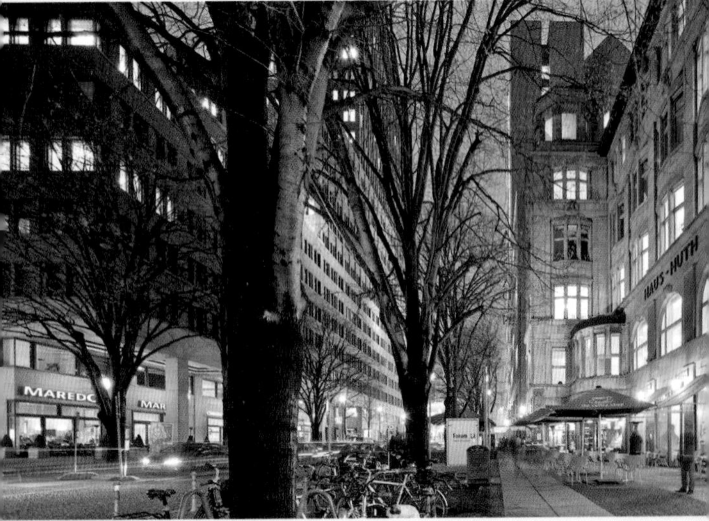

Alte Potsdamer Strasse by night

Don't Miss

Panoramapunkt

Europe's fastest **lift** (030-2593 7080; www.panoramapunkt.de; adult/concession €6.50/5, without wait €10.50/8; 10am-8pm, last ride 7.30pm, reduced hours in winter) yo-yos up and down the red-brick postmodern Kollhof Building. From the 100m viewing platform, a stunning 360-degree panorama reveals the city's layout. Study key moments in Potsdamer Platz history by taking in the exhibit, then relax in the on-site cafe.

Sony Center

Helmut Jahn's visually dramatic **Sony Center** (Potsdamer Strasse) is fronted by a 26-floor glass-and-steel tower that integrates rare relics from the pre-war Potsdamer Platz. These include a section of facade of the Hotel Esplanade and the opulent Kaisersaal hall, whose 75m move to its current location required some wizardly technology.

Museum für Film und Fernsehen

This Sony Center **museum** (030-300 9030; www.deutsche-kinemathek.de; adult/concession €7/4.50; 10am-6pm Tue, Wed & Fri-Sun, to 8pm Thu) charts milestones in German film and TV history. Most engaging are the galleries dedicated to pioneers such as Fritz Lang, ground-breaking movies such as Leni Riefenstahl's *Olympia,* German exiles in Hollywood and diva extraordinaire Marlene Dietrich.

Weinhaus Huth

The 1912 Weinhaus Huth, one of the first steel-frame buildings in town, was the only Potsdamer Platz structure to survive WWII intact. The **Daimler Contemporary** (030-2594 1420; www.sammlung.daimler.com; Weinhaus Huth, Alte Potsdamer Strasse 5, 4th fl; admission free; 11am-6pm) showcases international abstract, conceptual and minimalist art. Ring the bell to be buzzed in.

Top Tips

- Check out the Berlin Wall segments outside the Potsdamer Platz station entrance.
- Keep an eye out for public sculptures by Keith Haring, Robert Rauschenberg and other contemporary artists.
- For fantastic Italian ice cream head to Caffé & Gelato in the Potsdamer Platz Arkaden.
- From September to June, free classical concerts are held at 1pm Tuesday at the nearby Berliner Philharmonie.
- For celeb-spotting, visit in February when Potsdamer Platz hosts the Berlinale film festival.

Take a Break

Report to Qiu (p68) for a sit-down lunch in stylish surroundings.

Short on time? Try the food-court-style eateries in the basement of the Potsdamer Platz Arkaden.

Top Sights
Jüdisches Museum

In a landmark building by American-Polish architect Daniel Libeskind, Berlin's Jewish Museum offers a chronicle of trials and triumphs in 2000 years of German-Jewish history. The exhibit smoothly navigates through all major periods, from the Romans and the Middle Ages to the Age of Enlightenment and the community's renaissance today. Find out about Jewish cultural contributions, holiday traditions, the difficult road to emancipation and outstanding individuals such as philosopher Moses Mendelssohn, jeans inventor Levi Strauss and painter Felix Nussbaum.

Map p64, E4

www.jmberlin.de

Lindenstrasse 9-14

adult/concession €8/3

10am-10pm Mon, to 8pm Tue-Sun, last admission 1hr before closing

S Hallesches Tor, Kochstrasse

Daniel Libeskind's Jüdisches Museum

)on't Miss

'he Building

•aniel Libeskind's stunning structure is essen-ıally a 3D metaphor for the tortured history of he Jewish people. Its zigzag outline symbolises broken Star of David; its silvery zinc walls are harply angled; and instead of windows there are nly small gashes piercing the gleaming facade.

ıxes

'he visual allegory continues inside, where a teep staircase descends to three intersecting ʋalkways – called 'axes' – representing the fates f Jews during the Nazi years: death, exile and ontinuity. Only the latter leads to the exhibit.

;chalechet (Fallen Leaves)

Ienashe Kadishman's art installation is one of he museum's most poignant. More than 10,000 pen-mouthed faces cut from rusty iron plates e scattered on the floor in an ocean of silent creams. The space itself, a claustrophobic ement-walled enclosure that Libeskind calls a Iemory Void, is a metaphor for the loss of the ıurdered Jews of Europe.

Ioses Mendelssohn Exhibit

'hilosopher Moses Mendelssohn (1729–86) was key figure in the Jewish Enlightenment. His ›rogressive thinking and lobbying paved the way ɔr the Emancipation Edict of 1812, which made ews full Prussian citizens with equal rights.

Iax Liebermann Self-Portrait

Iax Liebermann (1847–1935) was Germany's ıost famous impressionist, and co-founder of the ;erlin Secession movement. This painting shows he Jewish artist as an old man in 1929, wearing is signature Panama hat.

Top Tips

- Rent the audioguide (€3) for a more in-depth experience.
- Tickets are also valid for reduced admission on the same and the next two days to the Berlinische Galerie, an excellent survey of nearly 150 years of Berlin art, just 500m away.
- Themed tours take place at 3pm on Saturdays and Sundays (German only).

Take a Break

The museum's **Cafe Schmus** (☎030-2579 6751; www.koflerkompanie.com; Lindenstrasse 9-14; dishes €5.50-8; ⏰10am-10pm Mon, 10am-8pm Tue-Sun) serves modern takes on traditional Jewish cuisine, extending into the courtyard in summer.

Alternatively, head to the edgily designed **Cafe Dix** (mains €2.50-10; ⏰10am-7pm Wed-Mon) in the Berlinische Galerie for salads, German dishes and cake.

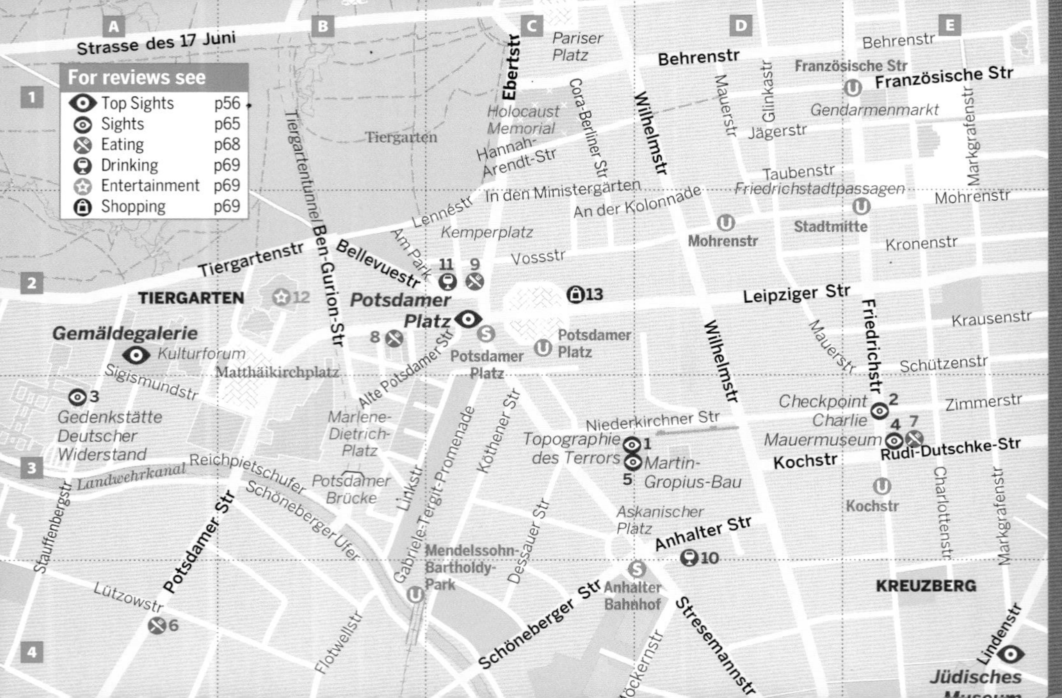
For reviews see
Top Sights p56
Sights p65
Eating p68
Drinking p69
Entertainment p69
Shopping p69
A
B
C
D
E
1
2
3
4
Strasse des 17 Juni
Tiergarten
Tiergartentunnel
Ben-Gurion-Str
Tiergartenstr
TIERGARTEN
12
Gemäldegalerie
Kulturforum
Matthäikirchplatz
Sigismundstr
3
Gedenkstätte Deutscher Widerstand
Landwehrkanal
Reichpietschufer
Schöneberger Ufer
Potsdamer Brücke
Marlene-Dietrich-Platz
Alte Potsdamer Str
Potsdamer Platz
8
11
9
Bellevuestr
Am Park
Lennéstr
Kemperplatz
Ebertstr
Holocaust Memorial
Hannah-Arendt-Str
In den Ministergärten
An der Kolonnade
Vossstr
13
Pariser Platz
Cora-Berliner Str
Wilhelmstr
Behrenstr
Mauerstr
Glinkastr
Jägerstr
Taubenstr
Friedrichstadtpassagen
Mohrenstr
Stadtmitte
Französische Str
Gendarmenmarkt
Markgrafenstr
Kronenstr
Krausenstr
Leipziger Str
Schützenstr
Zimmerstr
Friedrichstr
Checkpoint Charlie
2
Mauermuseum
4
7
Kochstr
Rudi-Dutschke-Str
Charlottenstr
KREUZBERG
Lindenstr
Jüdisches
Niederkirchner Str
Topographie des Terrors
1
Martin-Gropius-Bau
5
Askanischer Platz
Anhalter Str
10
Anhalter Bahnhof
Stresemannstr
Schöneberger Str
Dessauer Str
Köthener Str
Gabriele-Tergit-Promenade
Linkstr
Mendelssohn-Bartholdy-Park
Flottwellstr
Potsdamer Str
Lützowstr
6
Stauffenbergstr

Plaque, Checkpoint Charlie

›ights

'opographie des 'errors

MEMORIAL

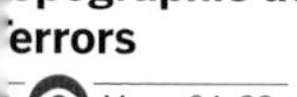
Map p64, C3

ı the same spot where once stood ıe most feared institutions of Nazi ›ermany (including the Gestapo eadquarters and the SS central ›mmand), this compelling exhibit ıronicles the stages of terror and ersecution, puts a face on the perpe-:ators and details the impact these rutal institutions had on all of Eur-pe. A second exhibit outside zeroes ı on how life changed for Berlin and s people after the Nazis made it their ıpital. (Topography of Terror; 030-2548 0950; www.topographie.de; Niederkirchner Strasse 8; admission free; 10am-8pm, grounds until dusk or 8pm latest; ; S Potsdamer Platz, Potsdamer Platz)

Checkpoint Charlie

HISTORIC SITE

2 Map p64, E3

Checkpoint Charlie was the principal gateway for foreigners and diplomats between the two Berlins from 1961 to 1990. Unfortunately, this potent symbol of the Cold War has become a tacky tourist trap, although a free open-air exhibit that illustrates milestones in Cold War history is one redeeming aspect. (cnr Zimmerstrasse & Friedrichstrasse; 24hr; S Kochstrasse, Stadtmitte)

Gedenkstätte Deutscher Widerstand MEMORIAL

3 Map p64, A3

This important exhibit on German Nazi resistance occupies the very rooms where high-ranking officers led by Claus Schenk Graf von Stauffenberg plotted the assassination attempt on Hitler on 20 July 1944. There's a memorial in the courtyard where the main conspirators were shot right after the failed coup, a story poignantly retold in the 2008 movie *Valkyrie*. (German Resistance Memorial Center; ☎030-2699 5000; www.gdw-berlin.de; Stauffenbergstrasse 13-14; admission free ⏰9am-6pm Mon-Wed & Fri, 9am-8pm Thu, 10am-6pm Sat & Sun; M29, S Potsdamer Platz, Kurfürstenstrasse, Potsdamer Platz)

Top Tip

Kulturforum Museums

In addition to the **Gemäldegalerie** (p56) and the **Neue Nationalgalerie** (which is closed for renovations), the Kulturforum encompasses three other top-rated museums: the **Kupferstichkabinett** (Map p64, A3; Gallery of Prints and Drawing; www.smb.museum/kk; Matthäikirchplatz), with prints and drawings dating from the 14th century; the **Musikinstrumenten-Museum** (Map p64, B2; Musical Instruments Museum; www.mim-berlin.de; Tiergartenstrasse 1), with rare historical instruments; and the **Kunstgewerbemuseum** (Map p64, A2; Museum of Decorative Art; www.smb.museum; Matthäikirchplatz), with its prized collection of arts and crafts. 'Area tickets' are valid at multiple museums on the same day.

Mauermuseum MUSEUM

4  Map p64, E3

The Cold War years, especially the history and horror of the Berlin Wall, are engagingly, if haphazardly, documented in this privately run tourist magnet. Open since 1961, the aging exhibition is still strong when it comes to telling the stories of escape attempts to the West. Original devices used in the process, including a hot-air balloon, a one-person submarine and a BMW Isetta, are crowd favourites. (Haus am Checkpoint Charlie; ☎030-253 7250; www.mauermuseum.de; Friedrichstrasse 43-45; adult/concession €12.50/9.50; ⏰9am-10pm; S Kochstrasse)

Martin-Gropius-Bau GALLERY

5  Map p64, C3

With its mosaics, terracotta reliefs and airy atrium, this Italian Renaissance-style exhibit space named for its architect (Walter Gropius' great-uncle) is a celebrated venue for high-calibre travelling shows. Whether it's a David Bowie retrospective, the latest works of Ai Weiwei or an ethnological exhibit on the mysteries of Angkor Wat, it's bound to be well curated and utterly fascinating. (☎030-254 860; www.gropiusbau.de; Niederkirchner Strasse 7; cost varies; ⏰10am-7pm Wed-Mon; S Potsdamer Platz, Potsdamer Platz)

Understand

The Berlin Wall

It's more than a tad ironic that Berlin's most popular tourist attraction is one that no longer exists. For 28 years the Berlin Wall, the most potent symbol of the Cold War, divided not only a city but the world.

The Beginning

Shortly after midnight on 13 August 1961, East German soldiers and police began rolling out miles of barbed wire that would soon be replaced with prefabricated concrete slabs. The Wall was a desperate measure launched by the German Democratic Republic (GDR) government to stop the sustained brain and brawn drain the country had experienced since its 1949 founding. Some 3.6 million people had already headed to western Germany, putting the GDR on the brink of economic and political collapse.

The Physical Border

Euphemistically called the 'Anti-Fascist Protection Barrier', the Berlin Wall was continually reinforced and refined. In the end, it was a complex border-security system consisting of two walls enclosing a 'death strip' riddled with trenches, floodlights, attack dogs, electrified alarm fences and watchtowers staffed by guards with shoot-to-kill orders.

Nearly 100,000 GDR citizens tried to escape, many using spectacular contraptions like homemade hot-air balloons or U-boats. There are no exact numbers, but it is believed that hundreds died in the process.

The End

The Wall's demise came as unexpectedly as its creation. Once again the GDR was losing its people in droves, this time via Hungary, which had opened its borders with Austria. Major demonstrations in East Berlin came to a head in early November 1989 when half a million people gathered on Alexanderplatz. Something had to give. It did on 9 November, when a GDR spokesperson mistakenly announced during a press conference on live TV that all travel restrictions to the West would be lifted immediately. Amid scenes of wild partying, the two Berlins came together again.

Today, only about 2km of the hated barrier still stands, most famously the 1.3km-long East Side Gallery. In addition, a double row of cobblestones embedded in the pavement and 30 information panels guide visitors along 5.7km of the Wall's course.

Eating

Joseph-Roth-Diele GERMAN €

6 Map p64, A4

Named for an Austrian Jewish writer, this wood-panelled saloon time-warps you back to the 1920s, when Roth used to live next door. Walls decorated with bookshelves and quotations from his works draw a literary, chatty crowd, especially at lunchtime. There's only four or five German home-cooking classics on the daily-changing menu. Pay at the counter. (030-2636 9884; www.joseph-roth-diele.de; Potsdamer Strasse 75; dishes €4-10; 10am-midnight Mon-Fri; S Kurfürstenstrasse)

Berliner Philharmonie

Restaurant Tim Raue ASIAN €€€

7 Map p64, E3

Now here's a twin-Michelin-starred restaurant we can get our mind around. Unstuffy ambience and subtly sophisticated design pair perfectly with Raue's brilliant Asian-inspired plates that each shine the spotlight on a few choice ingredients. Various taste sensations – sweet and salty, mild and hot – play off each other in perfect harmony. The Peking duck is a perennial bestseller. Popular at lunchtime too. (030-2593 7930; www.tim-raue.com; Rudi-Dutschke-Strasse 26; 3-/4-course lunch €38/48, 4-/6-course dinner €118/158; noon-3pm & 7pm-midnight Tue-Sat; S Kochstrasse)

Qiu INTERNATIONAL €€

8 Map p64, B2

The two-course business lunch at this stylish lounge also includes soup or salad, a non-alcoholic beverage and coffee or tea. We call that a steal. (030-590 051 230; www.qiu.de; Mandala Hotel, Potsdamer Strasse 3; 2-course lunch €14; business lunch noon-3pm Mon-Fri; 200, S Potsdamer Platz, Potsdamer Platz)

Vapiano ITALIAN €

9 Map p64, C2

Matteo Thun's jazzy decor is a great foil for the tasty Italian fare at this successful German self-service chain. Mix-and-match pastas, creative salads and crusty pizzas are all prepared right before your eyes, and there's fresh basil on the table. Your order is recorded on chip card and paid for upon leaving. ıere's another branch in Charlotten- ırg at Augsburger Strasse 4. (☎030- 00 5005; www.vapiano.de; Potsdamer Platz mains €5.50-10; ⏰10am-1am Mon-Sat, am-midnight Sun; 🚌200, S Potsdamer ıtz, U Potsdamer Platz)

›rinking

olar BAR

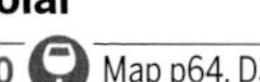
0 Map p64, D3

'atch the city light up from this 17th- ›or glass-walled sky lounge above a ›sh restaurant (mains €18 to €29). ith its dim lighting, soft black leather uches and breathtaking views, it's a eat spot for a date or sunset drinks. 'en getting there aboard an exterior ass lift is half the fun. Enter via the ıunky high-rise behind the Pit Stop ıto shop. (☎0163 765 2700; www.solar- rlin.de; Stresemannstrasse 76; ⏰6pm-2am ın-Thu, to 4am Fri & Sat; U Anhalter Bahnhof)

urtain Club BAR

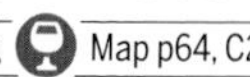
1 Map p64, C2

'ery night at 6pm, it's showtime at the tz-Carlton Berlin: a uniformed former ›efeater (Tower of London guard) remoniously pulls back the heavy cur- ıns on this elegant, wood-panelled bar esided over by cocktail-meister Arnd ›issen, who has created his own range perfume-inspired cocktails, each rved in a unique glass. (☎030-337 776 196; www.ritzcarlton.de; Ritz-Carlton Berlin, Potsdamer Strasse 3; ⏰from 6pm; 🚌200, S Potsdamer Platz, U Potsdamer Platz)

Entertainment

Berliner Philharmonie CLASSICAL MUSIC

12  Map p64, B2

This world-famous concert hall has supreme acoustics and, thanks to Hans Scharoun's clever terraced vineyard design, not a bad seat in the house. It's the home turf of the Berliner Philharmoniker, which will be led by Sir Simon Rattle until 2018. Chamber music concerts take place at the adjacent **Kammermusiksaal**. (☎tickets 030-2548 8301; www.berliner-philharmoniker.de; Herbert-von-Karajan-Strasse 1; 🚌200, S Potsdamer Platz, U Potsdamer Platz)

Shopping

LP12 Mall of Berlin SHOPPING MALL

13  Map p64, C2

This spanking new retail quarter is tailor-made for black-belt mall rats. More than 270 stores vie for your shopping euros, including flagship stores by Karl Lagerfeld, Hugo Boss, Liebeskind, Muji and other high-end brands. (www.mallofberlin.de; Leipziger Platz 12; 🚌200, S Potsdamer Platz, U Potsdamer Platz)

Local Life
An Afternoon in the Bergmannkiez

Getting There

The Bergmannkiez is in the western part of Kreuzberg.

U U-Bahn To start the itinerary, get off at Gneisenaustrasse (U7). When you've finished, Mehringdamm station (U7) is closest.

One of Berlin's most charismatic neighbourhoods, the Bergmannkiez in gentrified western Kreuzberg is named for its main shopping strip, the Bergmannstrasse, which is chock-a-block with people-watching cafes and indie shops and boutiques. Nearby Tempelhof Airport saw its finest hour during the 1948–49 Berlin Blockade and is now a vast urban park. Above it all 'soars' the Kreuzberg hill, Berlin's highest natural elevation and a wonderful summertime play zone.

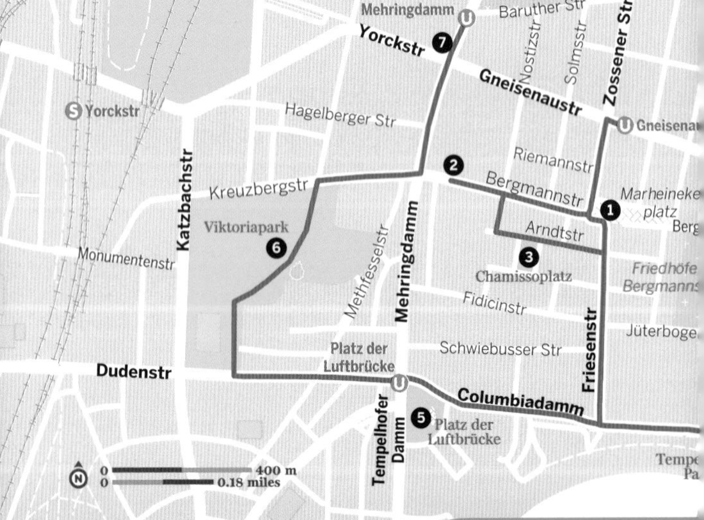

1 Marheineke Markthalle

hanks to a substantial renovation, ıe historic **Marheineke Markthalle** www.meine-markthalle.de; Marheinekeplatz; 8am-8pm Mon-Fri, 8am-6pm Sat; S Gneienaustrasse) has traded its grungy 19th-entury charm for bright and modern igs. Its aisles now brim with vendors lying everything from organic sausges to handmade cheeses, artisanal ıoney and other delicious bounty.

2 Colours

'intage fans love **Colours** (030-694 348; www.kleidermarkt.de; Bergmannstrasse 02, 1st fl; 11am-7pm Mon-Fri, noon-7pm at; S Mehringdamm), a huge loft of used lothing going back to the 1960s and vith a smaller selection of new street-nd club-wear threads, all priced by he kilo. Enter via the courtyard.

3 Chamissoplatz

Vith its ornate townhouses, cobbled treets, old-timey lanterns and even ın octagonal *pissoir*, **Chamissoplatz** S Platz der Luftbrücke) looks virtually ınchanged since the late 19th century, vhich is why this square is often used ıs a film set. An organic farmers maret takes place on Saturdays.

4 Tempelhofer Park

)ecomissioned Tempelhof Airport, vhich so gloriously handled the Berlin ıirlift of 1948–49, has been repurosed as a vast untamed urban **park** 030-2801 8162; www.tempelhoferfreiheit.e; enter via Oderstrasse, Tempelhofer Damm or Columbiadamm; sunrise to sunset; S Paradestrasse, Boddinstrasse, Leinestrasse). It's a wonderfully noncommercial, creative, open-sky space with a beer garden, art installations, urban gardening, barbecue areas and other fun zones. Enter from Columbiadamm.

5 Luftbrückendenkmal

The **Berlin Airlift Memorial** (Platz der Luftbrücke; S Platz der Luftbrücke) outside the former Tempelhof Airport honours those who participated in keeping the city fed and free during the 1948–49 Berlin Blockade. The trio of spikes represents the three air corridors used by the Western Allies, while the plinth bears the names of the 79 people who died in this colossal effort.

6 Viktoriapark

Take a break in this rambling park draped over the 66m-high Kreuzberg hill, home to a vineyard, a waterfall and a pompous memorial commemorating Napoleon's 1815 defeat. In summer, laid-back locals arrive to chill, tan or enjoy beers at **Golgatha** (030-785 2453; www.golgatha-berlin.de; Dudenstrasse 48-64; from 9am Apr-Sep; S Platz der Luftbrücke, R Yorckstrasse).

7 Curry 36

Day after day, night after night, a motley crowd – cops, cabbies, queens, office jockeys, savvy tourists etc – wait their turn at **Curry 36** (p109), a top *Currywurst* purveyor that's been frying 'em up since 1981.

Explore

Scheunenviertel

The Scheunenviertel (Barn Quarter) is one of Berlin's oldest, most charismatic neighbourhoods. Embark on an aimless wander and you'll constantly stumble upon enchanting surprises: here an idyllic courtyard or bleeding-edge gallery, there a fashion-forward boutique or belle époque ballroom. Since reunification, the Scheunenviertel has also reprised its historic role as Berlin's main Jewish Quarter.

ʼhe Sights in a Day

Make your way to Nordbahnhof S-Bahn station to start the day ʼith an in-depth study of the Berlin Wall ː the **Gedenkstätte Berliner Mauer** ɔ74). Follow Bernauer Strasse east to ᵎrunnenstrasse, then either walk south ast galleries, boutiques and cafes, or op on the U8 for the one-stop ride to osenthaler Platz and lunch at **District ɬôt** (p82).

Spend the afternoon rambling around the Scheunenviertel nd sourcing Berlin fashions and ccessories in the **Hackesche Höfe** ɔ78) and along Alte Schönhauser ᵎtrasse, Neue Schönhauser Strasse, ɬünzstrasse, Rosenthaler Strasse and ɿeir side streets. Get your art fix at **ːW Institute for Contemporary Art** ɔ81) and follow up with a strong cuppa ı its courtyard Café Bravo. Interested ı Berlin's Jewish community? Swing y the **Neue Synagoge** (p78) and the **ɬlter Jüdischer Friedhof** (p81).

Make dinner reservations at **Katz Orange** (p81) or **Pauly ᵎaal** (p81) for modern German fare. ᵎrab a cocktail at **Butcher's** (p83), ɦen hit the dance floor at the endear-ıgly retro **Clärchens Ballhaus** (p83).

Top Sight

Gedenkstätte Berliner Mauer (p74)

Best of Berlin

Eating

Katz Orange (p81)

Pauly Saal (p81)

Muret La Barba (p83)

Shopping

Bonbonmacherei (p84)

Butterflysoulfire (p85)

Ampelmann Galerie (p85)

Getting There

Bus The 142 runs along Torstrasse.

S S-Bahn Hackescher Markt station (S5, S7, S9) puts you in the thick of the Scheunenviertel. The S1, S2 and S25 stop at Nordbahnhof and Oranienburger Strasse.

Tram The M1 links key spots within the Scheunenviertel and goes up to Prenzlauer Berg.

U U-Bahn Weinmeisterstrasse (U8) is the most central station. Rosenthaler Platz (U8) and Rosa-Luxemburg-Platz (U2) are closer to Torstrasse and the northern Scheunenviertel.

Top Sights
Gedenkstätte Berliner Mauer

Few streets have played such a pivotal role in Cold War history as Bernauer Strasse. The Berlin Wall ran along its entire length, with one side in the east, the other in the west. Extending for 1.4km and integrating an original Wall segment, this memorial strives to explain how all the elements of the Wall and the death strip fit together, how the border fortifications were enlarged and perfected over time and what impact they had on the daily lives of people on both sides of the wall.

Map p76, C2

www.berliner-mauer-gedenkstaette.de

admission free

visitor center 9.30am 7pm Apr-Oct, to 6pm Nov-Mar

Nordbahnhof, Bernaue Strasse, Eberswalder Strasse

Window of Remembrance

Don't Miss

National Monument to German Division

The central memorial consists of a 70m section of original wall bounded by two rusted steel flanks. Behind it is a reconstructed 'death strip' complete with a guard tower, a security patrol path and the lamps that bathed it in fierce light at night.

Berliner Mauer Dokumentationszentrum

This recently revamped exhibit uses photographs, recordings and archival documents to provide a historical overview of Wall events.

Kapelle der Versöhnung

The simple but radiant Chapel of Reconciliation stands on the spot of an 1894 brick church detonated in 1985 to make room for a widening of the border strip.

Window of Remembrance

A wall of photographic portraits gives identity to the would-be escapees who lost their lives at the Berlin Wall. The parklike area surrounding the installation was once part of the adjacent cemetery.

Nordbahnhof 'Ghost Station'

The Wall divided the city's transportation system. Three train lines that originated in West Berlin had to travel beneath East Berlin before returning to the western side. At heavily guarded 'ghost-stations', trains slowed but did not stop; one of them, today's S-Bahn station Nordbahnhof, has an exhibit on the subject.

Tunnel 29

A highlight between Brunnenstrasse and Schwedter Strasse is a display on the world-famous Tunnel 29, which ran for 135m below Bernauer Strasse and helped 29 people escape from East Berlin in September 1962.

☑ Top Tips

- ▶ The visitor centre has free maps and screens a short introductory film.
- ▶ Enjoy sweeping views of the memorial from the viewing tower near Ackerstrasse.
- ▶ A 15-minute remembrance service for the Wall victims is held in the Chapel of Reconciliation at noon Tuesday to Friday.
- ▶ The open-air exhibit is open from 8am till 10pm.

✕ Take a Break

The friendly if tourist-oriented **Ost-West Cafe** (Map p76, F3; ☎030-4677 6016; www.ost-west-cafe.de; Brunnenstrasse 53; mains €4-7; ⏱8am-10pm; S Bernauer Strasse) serves simple international dishes amid Cold War–era-themed decor. It's about 600m from the Gedenkstätte Berliner Mauer, up Bernauer Strasse, on the corner of Brunnenstrasse.

A B C D

1 2 3 4 5

Bernauer Str
Ackerstr
Bergstr
S Nordbahnhof
Gedenkstätte Berliner Mauer
Gartenstr
Bergstr
Chausseestr
Habersaathstr
Invalidenstr
Naturkundemuseum
Museum für Naturkunde
5
4
Invalidenstr
Eichendorffstr
Schlegelstr
Tieckstr
Gartenstr
Novalisstr
Hannoversche Str
14
KW Institu
Contempora
Hessische Str
Linienstr
Jüdische Mädchenschule
Oranienburger Tor
Auguststr
9
22
Heckmann Höfe
Oranienburger Str
Luisenstr
Friedrichstr
Neue Synagoge
Johannisstr
Tucholskystr
Sammlung Boros
Schumannstr
Albrechtstr
3
Reinhardtstr
21
Kalkscheunenstr
Ziegelstr
Mon

For reviews see

Top Sights	p74
Sights	p78
Eating	p81
Drinking	p83
Entertainment	p84
Shopping	p84

E
F
G
H
1
2
3
4
5
0
400 m
0
0.2 miles
Ruppinerstr
Anklamer Str
Fehrbelliner Str
Zionskirchplatz
Kastanienallee
Schönhauser Allee
Brunnenstr
Schwedter Str
Veteranenstr
Volkspark am Weinbergsweg
Weinbergsweg
Choriner Str
Senefelderplatz
Teutoburger Platz
Schönhauser Allee
Rosenthaler Platz
Torstr
17
Rosenthaler Str
Torstr
Linienstr
Linienstr
18
Koppenplatz
19
Auguststr
25
12
15
Mulackstr
Rosa-Luxemburg-Platz
11
Gipsstr
Grosse Hamburger Str
Gormannstr
Steinstr
Alte Schönhauser Str
Max-Beer-Str
Almstadtstr
Hirtenstr
Weydinger Str
Sophie-Gips-Höfe
Sophienstr
Weinmeisterstr
13
23
24
Alter Jüdischer Friedhof
7
Hackesche Höfe
Neue Schönhauser Str
Münzstr
Rosa-Luxemburg-Str
Prenzlauer Allee
1
20
Memhardstr
Monbijouplatz
Monbijou Park
Dircksenstr

Sights

Hackesche Höfe

HISTORIC SITE

1 Map p76, F5

Thanks to its congenial mix of cafes, galleries, boutiques and entertainment venues, this attractively restored complex of eight interlinked courtyards is hugely popular with the tourist brigade. **Court I**, festooned with patterned art nouveau tiles, is the prettiest. **Court VII** leads off to the romantic **Rosenhöfe**, a single courtyard with a sunken rose garden and tendril-like balustrades. (030-2809 8010; www.hackesche-hoefe.com; Rosenthaler Strasse 40/41, Sophienstrasse 6; admission free; M1, Hackescher Markt)

Neue Synagoge

SYNAGOGUE

Map p76, D5

The original New Synagogue, finished in 1866 in what was then the predominantly Jewish part of the city, was Germany's largest synagogue at that time. It was destroyed in WWII and rebuilt after the Berlin Wall fell. Now this space doubles as a museum and cultural centre documenting local Jewish life. (030-8802 8300; www.centrumjudaicum.de; Oranienburger Strasse 28-30; adult/concession €3.50/3, dome €2/1.50; 10am-8pm Sun & Mon, to 6pm Tue-Thu, to 5pm Fri, shorter hours Oct-Mar; S Oranienburger Tor, Oranienburger Strasse)

Sammlung Boros

GALLERY

3 Map p76, B5

This Nazi-era bunker shelters one of Berlin's finest private collections of contemporary art. Advertising guru Christian Boros acquired the behemoth in 2003 and converted it into a shining beacon of art. Book online (months ahead, if possible) to join a guided tour (also in English) of works by such hot shots as Wolfgang Tilmanns, Olafur Eliasson and Ai Weiwei and to pick up fascinating nuggets about the building's colourful past as a tropical-fruit warehouse and techno and fetish club. (Boros Collection; 030-2759 4065; www.sammlung-boros.de; Reinhardtstrasse 20; adult/concession €12/6; tours 3-8pm Thu, 10am-8pm Fri, 10am-6pm Sat & Sun; S Oranienburger Tor, Friedrichstrasse, M1, Friedrichstrasse)

Hamburger Bahnhof – Museum für Gegenwart

MUSEUM

4 Map p76, A3

Berlin's main contemporary art museum opened in 1996 in an old railway station, whose loft and grandeur are a great backdrop for this Aladdin's cave of paintings, installations, sculptures and video art. Changing exhibits span the arc of post-1950 artistic endeavour – Conceptual Art, Pop Art, Minimal Art, Fluxus – and often feature seminal works by such key players as Andy Warhol, Cy Twombly, Joseph Beuys and Robert Rauschenberg. (030-266 424 242; www.hamburgerbahnhof.de; Invalidenstrasse 50-51; adult/concession €10/5; 10am-6pm

Neue Synagoge

Tue, Wed & Fri, to 8pm Thu, 11am-6pm Sat & Sun; S Hauptbahnhof, Hauptbahnhof)

Museum für Naturkunde MUSEUM

5 Map p76, A3

Fossils and minerals don't quicken your pulse? Well, how about the world's largest mounted dino? The 12m-high *Brachiosaurus branchai* is joined by a dozen other Jurassic buddies, some of which are brought to virtual flesh-and-bone life with the help of clever 'Juraskopes'. Other crowd favourites include an ultrarare archaeopteryx and, hopefully soon, the world's most famous dead polar bear, Knut. (Museum of Natural History; 030-2093 8591; www.naturkunde-museum-berlin.de; Invalidenstrasse 43; adult/concession incl audioguide €5/3; 9.30am-6pm Tue-Sun; S Naturkundemuseum)

Jüdische Mädchenschule HISTORIC BUILDING

6 Map p76, D4

A 1920s former Jewish Girls' School reopened in 2012 as a cultural and culinary centre in a sensitively restored New Objectivity structure by Alexander Beer. Three renowned Berlin galleries – **Eigen+Art Lab**, **CWC** and **Michael Fuchs** – and the **Museum The Kennedys** have set up shop in the former classrooms, while the ground floor has the Jewish deli **Mogg &**

Understand

Jewish Berlin

Since reunification, Berlin has had the fastest-growing Jewish community in the world. It is diverse: most members are Russian Jewish immigrants but there are also Jews of German heritage, Israelis wishing to escape their politically frustrating homeland and American expats lured by Berlin's low-cost living and limitless creativity. Today there are about 13,000 active members of the Jewish community, including 1000 belonging to the Orthodox congregation Adass Yisroel. However, since not all Jews choose to be affiliated with a synagogue, the actual population is estimated to be at least twice as high.

Community Roots

Records show that Jews first settled in Berlin in 1295, but throughout the Middle Ages they had to contend with being blamed for any kind of societal or economic woe. When the plague struck (1348–49), rumours that Jews had poisoned the wells led to the first major pogrom. In 1510, 38 Jews were publicly tortured and burned for allegedly stealing the host from a church because a confession by the actual (Christian) perpetrator was deemed too straightforward to be true.

Financial interests, not humanitarian ones, motivated the Elector Friedrich Wilhelm to invite Jewish families expelled from Vienna to settle in Berlin in 1671. To his credit, he later extended the offer to Jews in general and also allowed them to practise their faith – which at the time was still considered a privilege throughout Europe.

The Last Century

By the late 19th century, many of Berlin's Jews, numbering about 5% of the city's population, had become thoroughly German in speech and identity. When a wave of Hasidic Jews escaping the pogroms of Eastern Europe arrived around the same time, they found their way to today's Scheunenviertel, which at that time was an immigrant slum with cheap housing. By 1933 Berlin's Jewish population had grown to around 160,000 and constituted one-third of all Jews living in Germany. The well-known horrors of the Nazi years sent most into exile and left 55,000 dead. Only 1000 to 2000 Jews are believed to have survived the war years in Berlin, often with the help of their non-Jewish neighbours.

Melzer (☎030-330 060 770; www.moggand-melzer.com; mains €7-15; ⏰8am-late Mon-Fri, 10am-late Sat & Sun) and the Michelin-starred Pauly Saal (p81). (www.maedchen-schule.org; Augustrasse 11-13; admission free; ⏰hours vary; S Oranienburger Tor, 🚋M1, 🚆Oranienburger Strasse)

Alter Jüdischer Friedhof

CEMETERY

7 Map p76, E5

What looks like a small park was in fact Berlin's first Jewish cemetery, destroyed by the Nazis in 1943. Some 12,000 people were buried here between 1672 and 1827, including the philosopher Moses Mendelssohn. His tombstone (not the original) stands representative for all the 6ft-under residents. (Grosse Hamburger Strasse; 🚋M1, 🚆Hackescher Markt)

KW Institute for Contemporary Art

GALLERY

8 Map p76, D4

In an old margarine factory, non-profit KW helped chart the fate of the Scheunenviertel as Berlin's original post-Wall art district. It still stages ground-breaking shows reflecting the latest – and often radical – trends in contemporary art. Free tours (with reduced admission) run Thursday at 7pm. KW's founders also inaugurated the **Berlin Biennale** (www.berlinbiennale.de) in 1998. The courtyard **Café Bravo** (☎030-2345 7777; www.bravomitte.de; ⏰9am-8pm Mon-Wed, Fri & Sat, to 9pm Thu, 10am-8pm Sun) makes for a stylish coffee break. (☎030-243 4590; www.kw-berlin.de; Augustrasse 69; adult/concession €6/4; ⏰noon-7pm Tue, Wed & Fri-Sun, to 9pm Thu; S Oranienburger Strasse, 🚋M1, 🚆Oranienburger Tor)

Eating

Pauly Saal

GERMAN €€€

9 Map p76, D4

Regionally hunted and gathered ingredients steer the seasonal menu of Michael Hoepfl, who needed only one year to coax a star from the Michelin testers for his earthy gourmet cuisine. Try the Pomeranian entrecôte amid 1920s inspired decor spiced up with provocative artwork. (☎030-3300 6070; www.paulysaal.com; Augustrasse 11-13; mains lunch €15-20, dinner €29-40; ⏰noon-3pm & 8pm-3am Mon-Sat; S Oranienburger Tor, 🚋M1, 🚆Oranienburger Strasse)

Katz Orange

INTERNATIONAL €€€

10 Map p76, D2

With its gourmet organic farm-to-table menu, feel-good country styling and swift and smiling servers, the 'Orange Cat' hits a gastro grand slam. It will have you purring for Duroc pork that's been slow-roasted for 12 hours giving extra-rich flavour. The setting in a castle-like former brewery is stunning, especially in summer when the patio opens. (☎030-983 208 430; www.katzorange.com; Bergstrasse 22; mains €18-26; ⏰6-11pm; S Rosenthaler Platz, 🚋M8)

Chèn Chè

VIETNAMESE €€

11 Map p76, F4

Settle down in the charming Zen garden or beneath the hexagonal chandelier of this exotic Vietnamese teahouse and pick from the small menu of steaming *pho* (soups), curries and noodle dishes served in traditional clay pots. Exquisite tea selection and small store. (www.chenche-berlin.de; Rosenthaler Strasse 13; mains €8-10; noon-midnight; ; S Rosenthaler Platz, M1)

District Môt

VIETNAMESE €

12 Map p76, F4

At this colourful mock-Saigon street-food parlour, patrons squat on tiny plastic stools around wooden tables where rolls of toilet paper irreverently stand in for paper napkins. The small-plate menu mixes the familiar (steamy *pho* noodle soup, papaya salad) with the adventurous (stewed eel, deep-fried silk worms). (030-2008 9284; www.districtmot.com; Rosenthaler Strasse 62; dishes €4-19; noon-1am Sun-Thu, to 2am Fri & Sat; S Rosenthaler Platz, M1)

AGENCJA FOTOGRAFICZNA CARO/ALAMY ©

Clärchens Ballhaus

Susuru

JAPANESE €

13 Map p76, H5

Go ye forth and slurp! *Susuru* is Japanese for slurping and, quite frankly, that's the best way to deal with the oodles of noodles at this soup parlour, which looks as neat and stylish as a bento box. (030-211 1182; www.susuru.de; Rosa-Luxemburg-Strasse 17; mains €6.50-9; 11.30am-11.30pm; ; S Rosa-Luxemburg-Platz)

Schwarzwaldstuben

GERMAN €€

14 Map p76, D4

In the mood for a Hansel and Gretel moment? Then join the other 'lost kids' for satisfying southern German food amid tongue-in-cheek forest decor. Thumbs up for the *Spätzle* (mac 'n' cheese), *Maultaschen* (ravioli-like pasta) and giant schnitzel, all best washed down with a crisp Rothaus Tannenzäpfle beer, straight from the Black Forest. (030-2809 8084; Tucholskystrasse 48; mains €7-14; 9am-midnight; M1, Oranienburger Strasse)

Muret La Barba

ITALIAN **€€**

15 Map p76, F4

This wine-shop-bar-restaurant combo oozes the kind of rustic authenticity that instantly transports cognoscenti to the Boot. The food is hearty, inventive, and made with top ingredients imported from the motherland. All wine is available by the glass or by the bottle (corkage fee €9.50). (030-2809 7212; www.muretlabarba.de; Rosenthaler Strasse 61; mains €9-19; 10am-midnight Mon-Fri, noon-midnight Sat & Sun; S Rosenthaler Platz)

Drinking

Clärchens Ballhaus

CLUB

16 Map p76, E4

Yesteryear is right now at this late, great 19th-century dance hall where groovers and grannies hoof it across the parquet without even a touch of irony. There's different sounds nightly – salsa to swing, tango to disco – and a live band on Saturday. (030-282 9295; www.ballhaus.de; Augustrasse 24; 11am-late, dancing from 9pm or 9.30pm; M1, Oranienburger Strasse)

Butcher's

BAR

17 Map p76, F3

Channelling PDT in New York, cocktail whisperer David Wiedemann has created a furtive libation station in a former butchershop entered via a red British phone booth tucked into a sausage parlour called Fleischerei. Drinks are expertly mixed and the ambience is refined, even if meat hooks, a leather bar and blood-red light play upon the place's early incarnation. (www.butcher-berlin.de; Torstrasse 116; 8.30pm-late Tue-Sat; S Rosenthaler Platz, M1)

Local Life

Rosenthaler Platz: Snack Central

For feeding hunger pangs on the quick and cheap, choices could not be greater than around **Rosenthaler Platz U-Bahn station** (Map p76, F3) Our three faves are **Rosenthaler Grill und Schlemmerbuffet** (030-283 2153; Torstrasse 125; dishes €2.80-7; 24hr) for Oscar-worthy doner kebabs, **Rosenburger** (030-2408 3037; Brunnenstrasse 196; burgers €3-6; 11am-3am Sun-Thu, to 5am Fri & Sat) for freshly made burgers, and **CôCô** (030-2463 0595; www.co-co.net; Rosenthaler Strasse 2; sandwiches €4.20-5.50; 11am-10pm Mon-Thu, to 11pm Fri & Sat, noon-10pm Sun) for bulging *banh mi* (Vietnamese sandwiches).

Kaffee Burger

CLUB

18 Map p76, H3

Nothing to do with either coffee or meat patties, this sweaty cult club with lovingly faded Commie-era decor is a fun-for-all concert and party pen with a sound policy that swings from indie and electro to klezmer punk without missing a beat. (☎030-2804 6495; www.kaffeeburger.de; Torstrasse 60; S Rosa-Luxemburg-Platz)

Amano Bar

BAR

19 Map p76, F4

This glamour vixen at the budget-hip Hotel Amano, with its marble bar, cubistic furnishings and warm chocolate hues, attracts chatty sophisticates with original libations that verge on cocktail alchemy. In summer, the action expands to the rooftop terrace. (☎030-809 4150; www.bar.hotel-amano.com; Augustrasse 43; 5pm-late; S Rosenthaler Platz, M1)

Entertainment

Chamäleon Varieté

CABARET

20 Map p76, F5

A marriage of art nouveau charms and high-tech theatre trappings, this intimate 1920s-style cabaret in an old ballroom presents classy variety shows – comedy, juggling acts and singing – often in sassy, sexy and unconventional fashion. (☎030-400 0590; www.chamaeleonberlin.com; Rosenthaler Strasse 40/41; M1, Hackescher Markt)

Friedrichstadtpalast

CABARET

21 Map p76, C5

Europe's largest revue theatre has a tradition going back to the 1920s and is famous for glitzy-glam Vegas-style productions with leggy showgirls, a high-tech stage, mind-boggling special effects and plenty of artistry. (☎030-2326 2326; www.palast-berlin.eu; Friedrichstrasse 107; S Oranienburger Tor, M1)

Shopping

Bonbonmacherei

FOOD

The aroma of peppermint and liquorice wafts through this old-fashioned

Understand

Scheunenviertel: From Hay to Hip

The Scheunenviertel's odd name (Barn Quarter) hearkens back centuries to the days of wooden houses, frequent fires and poor fire-fighting techniques, which is why the Prussian king ordered all barns containing flammable crops to be stored outside the city walls. In the early 20th century, the quarter absorbed huge numbers of poor Eastern European Jewish immigrants, many of whom were annihilated by the Nazis. After the war the Scheunenviertel gradually deteriorated into a down-at-heel East Berlin quarter, but it has catapulted from drab to fab since reunification. Now a creative-class darling, its cafes and bars brim with iPad-toters, sassy fashionistas and skinny stray artists.

basement candy kitchen whose owners use antique equipment and time-tested recipes to churn out such tasty treats as their signature leaf-shaped Berliner Maiblätter. (030-4405 5243; www.bonbonmacherei.de; Oranienburger Strasse 32, Heckmann Höfe; noon-8pm Wed-Sat Sep-Jun; M1, Oranienburger Strasse)

Ampelmann Galerie SOUVENIRS

23 Map p76, F5

It took a vociferous grassroots campaign to save the little Ampelmann, the endearing fellow on East German pedestrian traffic lights. Now the beloved cult figure and global brand graces an entire store worth of T-shirts, fridge magnets, pasta, onesies, umbrellas and other knick-knacks. (030-4472 6438; www.ampelmann.de; Court V, Hackesche Höfe, Rosenthaler Strasse 40/41; 9.30am-10pm Mon-Sat, 10am-7pm Sun; M1, Hackescher Markt)

1. Absinth Depot Berlin FOOD, DRINK

24 Map p76, G5

Van Gogh, Toulouse-Lautrec and Oscar Wilde were among the fin-de-siècle artists who drew inspiration from the 'green fairy', as absinthe is also known. This quaint little shop has over 100 varieties of the potent stuff and an expert owner who'll happily help you pick out the perfect bottle for your own mind-altering rendezvous. (030-281 6789; www.erstes-absinthdepotberlin.de; Weinmeisterstrasse 4; 2pm-midnight Mon-Fri, 1pm-midnight Sat; S Weinmeisterstrasse)

Local Life

Haus Schwarzenberg

The last holdout in the heavily gentrified area around the Hackescher Markt is **Haus Schwarzenberg** (Map p76, F5; www.haus-schwarzenberg.org; Rosenthaler Strasse 39; M1, Hackescher Markt). It's an unpretentious, authentic space where art and creativity are allowed to flourish beyond mainstream and commercial needs. Festooned with street art and bizarre metal sculptures, its courtyards lead to studios, offices, the Monsterkabinett 'amusement park', the edgy-arty bar Eschloraque Rümschrümp, an arthouse cinema and a trio of exhibits dealing with Jewish persecution during the Third Reich.

Butterflysoulfire FASHION

25 Map p76, G4

Only at the flagship store of Maria Thomas and Thoas Lindner's avant-garde Berlin fashion label can you get the latest cuts of cleverly geometric and asymmetric shirts, pants, jackets and basics. The eye-candy store also has deals and steals from last season, plus bags by Garnet, jewellery by Bjorg and other hipster items from small fashion-forward labels. (www.butterflysoulfire.com; Mulackstrasse 11; noon-8pm Mon-Sat; S Rosa-Luxemburg-Platz, Weinmeisterstrasse)

Explore

Kurfürstendamm

The glittering heart of West Berlin during the Cold War, Kurfürstendamm (aka Ku'damm) is nirvana for shopaholics, with fashionable boutiques mixing it up with high-street chains and department stores. Venture off the boulevard to sample the area's bourgeois charms, reflected in its palatial townhouses, distinctive shops, neighbourhood-adored restaurants, snazzy bars and old-style pubs.

The Sights in a Day

There will be a lot of walking today, so gather some strength with a bountiful breakfast at **Café-Restaurant Wintergarten im Literaturhaus** (p92), a darling neighbourhood cafe. Thus fortified, get the scoop on Berlin's tumultuous past at the **Story of Berlin** (p91), then launch an extended shopping spree down the boulevard, perhaps pausing to ponder the futility of war at the **Kaiser-Wilhelm-Gedächtniskirche** (p90). Check out the snazzy concept mall **Bikini Berlin** (p94), then swing down to the grand department store **KaDeWe** (p95) for a late lunch in the glorious food hall.

Do a bit more shopping if you must, or make your way to the **Museum für Fotografie** (p90) to look at Helmut Newton's nudes and whatever else is on view. Now it's practically beer-o'clock and the tables at **Dicke Wirtin** (p94) are singing their siren song.

A fine place for dinner is **Restaurant am Steinplatz** (p92) or, if you're in the mood for authentic Chinese, **Good Friends** (p92). Alternatively, catch a show and a bite in the stunning mirrored tent of **Bar Jeder Vernunft** (p95).

Best of Berlin

Shopping

Bikini Berlin (p94)

KaDeWe (p95)

Music & Performance

A-Trane (p95)

Bar Jeder Vernunft (p95)

Eating

Restaurant am Steinplatz (p92)

Bars

Monkey Bar (p94)

Museums

Museum für Fotografie (p90)

Clubs

Pearl (p95)

Getting There

Bus The M19, M29 and X10 travel along Kurfürstendamm.

S-Bahn Zoologischer Garten is the most central station.

U-Bahn The U1 stations Uhlandstrasse, Kurfürstendamm and Wittenbergplatz put you right into shopping central.

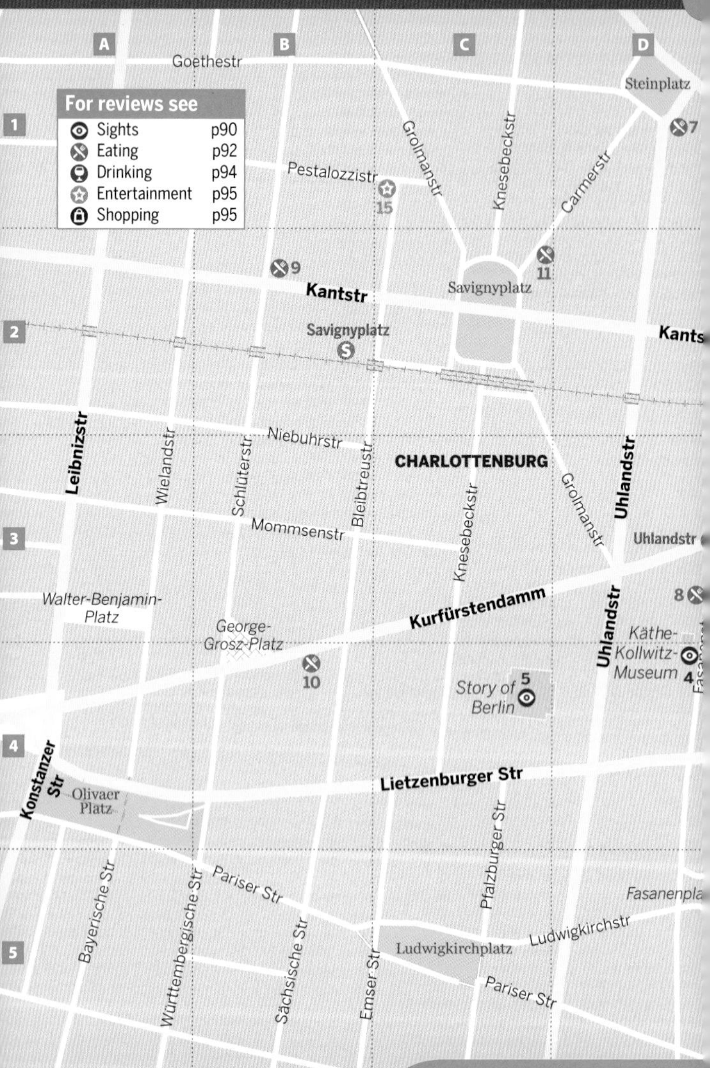
A
B
C
D
1
2
3
4
5
For reviews see
Sights p90
Eating p92
Drinking p94
Entertainment p95
Shopping p95
Goethestr
Steinplatz
Pestalozzistr
Grolmanstr
Knesebeckstr
Carmerstr
15
9
11
7
Kantstr
Savignyplatz
Savignyplatz
Kants
Niebuhrstr
CHARLOTTENBURG
Leibnizstr
Wielandstr
Schlüterstr
Bleibtreustr
Knesebeckstr
Grolmanstr
Uhlandstr
Mommsenstr
Uhlandstr
Walter-Benjamin-Platz
George-Grosz-Platz
Kurfürstendamm
8
Uhlandstr
Käthe-Kollwitz-Museum
4
10
Story of Berlin
5
Konstanzer Str
Olivaer Platz
Lietzenburger Str
Pfalzburger Str
Pariser Str
Fasanenpla
Bayerische Str
Württembergische Str
Sächsische Str
Emser Str
Ludwigkirchplatz
Ludwigkirchstr
Pariser Str

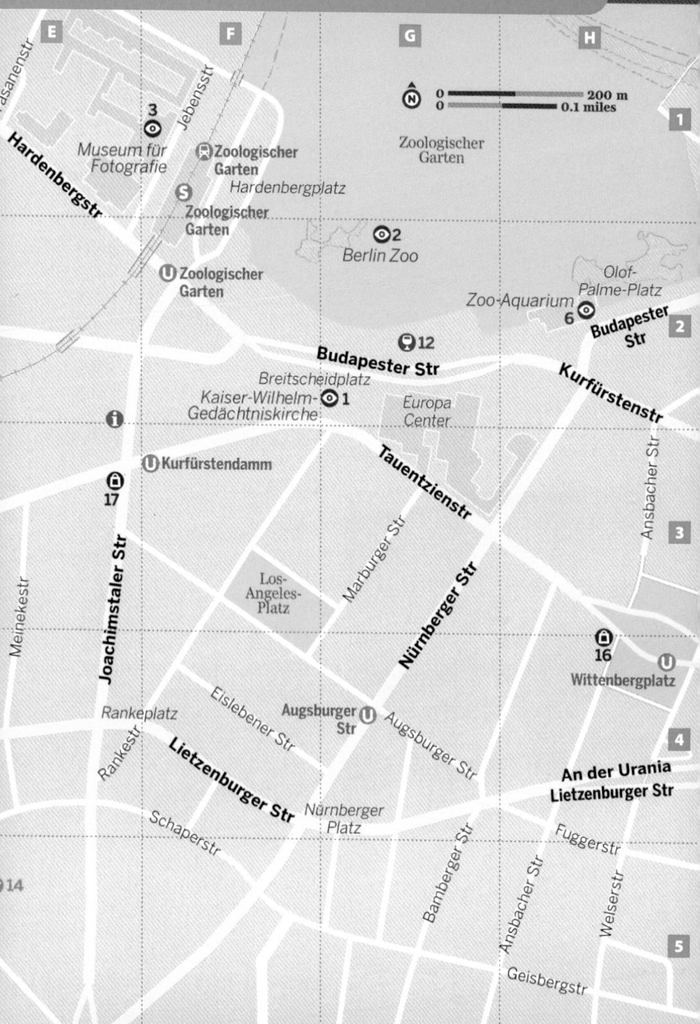

E
F
G
H
0 200 m
0 0.1 miles
1
2
3
4
5
Fasanenstr
Hardenbergstr
3
Museum für Fotografie
Jebensstr
Zoologischer Garten
Hardenbergplatz
Zoologischer Garten
Zoologischer Garten
Zoologischer Garten
2
Berlin Zoo
Olof-Palme-Platz
Zoo-Aquarium
6
Budapester Str
12
Budapester Str
Kurfürstenstr
Breitscheidplatz
Kaiser-Wilhelm-Gedächtniskirche
1
Europa Center
Kurfürstendamm
17
Tauentzienstr
Ansbacher Str
Joachimstaler Str
Meinekestr
Marburger Str
Los-Angeles-Platz
Nürnberger Str
16
Wittenbergplatz
Rankeplatz
Eislebener Str
Augsburger Str
Augsburger Str
Rankestr
Lietzenburger Str
An der Urania
Lietzenburger Str
Nürnberger Platz
Schaperstr
Fuggerstr
14
Bamberger Str
Ansbacher Str
Welserstr
Geisbergstr

Sights

Kaiser-Wilhelm-Gedächtniskirche CHURCH

 Map p88, G2

The bombed-out tower of this landmark church, consecrated in 1895, serves as an antiwar memorial, standing quiet and dignified amid the roaring traffic. The adjacent octagonal hall of worship, added in 1961, has amazing midnight-blue glass walls and a giant 'floating' Jesus. (Kaiser Wilhelm Memorial Church; 030-218 5023; www.gedaechtniskirche.com; Breitscheidplatz; admission free; church 9am-7pm, memorial hall 10am-6pm Mon-Fri, 10am-5.30pm Sat, noon-5.30pm Sun; 100, S Zoologischer Garten, Kurfürstendamm, Zoologischer Garten)

Humboldt penguin, Berlin Zoo

Berlin Zoo ZOO

2 Map p88, G2

Berlin's zoo holds a triple record as Germany's oldest, most species-rich and most popular animal park. It was established in 1844 under King Friedrich Wilhelm IV, who not only donated the land but also pheasants and other animals from the royal family's private reserve on the Pfaueninsel. The menagerie includes 20,000 critters representing 1500 species, including orangutans, koalas, rhinos, giraffes and penguins. (030-254 010; www.zoo-berlin.de; Hardenbergplatz 8; adult/child €13/6.50, with aquarium €20/10; 9am-7pm mid-Mar–Aug, 9am-6.30pm Sep & Oct, 9am-5pm Nov–mid-Mar; 100, 200, S Zoologischer Garten, Zoologischer Garten)

Museum für Fotografie MUSEUM

3 Map p88, F1

The artistic legacy of Helmut Newton (1920–2004), the Berlin-born *enfant terrible* of fashion and lifestyle photography, is given centre stage at Berlin's Photography Museum in a converted Prussian officers' casino behind Bahnhof Zoo. On the top floor, the gloriously restored barrel-vaulted **Kaisersaal** (Emperor's Hall) forms a grand backdrop for changing high-calibre photography exhibits drawn from the archive of the State Art Library. (030-266 424 242; www.smb.museum/mf; Jebensstrasse 2; adult/concession €10/5; 10am-6pm Tue,

Wed & Fri-Sun, 10am-8pm Thu; S Zoologischer Garten, Zoologischer Garten)

Käthe-Kollwitz-Museum MUSEUM

4 Map p88, D4

This exquisite museum is devoted to the artist Käthe Kollwitz (1867–1945), whose social and political awareness lent a tortured power to her lithographs, graphics, woodcuts, sculptures and drawings. Highlights include the antihunger lithography *Brot!* (Bread!; 1924) and the woodcut series *Krieg* (War; 1922–23). (030-882 5210; www.kaethe-kollwitz.de; Fasanenstrasse 24; adult/concession €6/3, audioguide €3; 11am-6pm; S Uhlandstrasse)

Story of Berlin MUSEUM

5 Map p88, C4

This multimedia museum breaks down 800 years of Berlin history into bite-size chunks that are easy to swallow but substantial enough to be satisfying. Each of the 23 rooms uses sound, light, technology and original objects to zero in on a specific theme or epoch in the city's history, from its founding in 1237 to the fall of the Berlin Wall. A creepily fascinating highlight is a tour (also in English) of a still functional atomic bunker beneath the building. (030-8872 0100; www.story-of-berlin.de; Kurfürstendamm 207-208, enter via Ku'damm Karree mall; adult/concession €12/9; 10am-8pm, last admission 6pm; S Uhlandstrasse)

Zoo-Aquarium AQUARIUM

6 Map p88, H2

Three floors of exotic fish, amphibians and reptiles await at this endearingly old-fashioned aquarium with its darkened halls and glowing tanks. Some of the specimens in the famous

Understand

C/O Reloaded

Displaced from its last location in a grand old postal centre on Oranienburger Strasse in Mitte, the nonprofit **C/O Berlin** (Map88, E2; 030-2844 4160; www.co-berlin.org; Hardenbergstrasse 22-14; S Bahnhof Zoologischer Garten, Bahnhof Zoologischer Garten), the city's most popular exhibition space for international photography, joined the westward migration and set up shop in the historic Amerika Haus near Zoo Station. The Amerika Haus was built in 1956–57 as part of the Interbau building exposition and served as a US culture and information centre, with a library, cinema and exhibition spaces. After the 1960s and '70s, when the building was pelted with eggs and rotten fruit during the anti–Vietnam War student protests, it became less and less accessible, turning into a virtual fortress after 9/11 and eventually closing down in September 2006. Plans to open a West Berlin museum here were ditched in favour of giving C/O a shiny new space.

Crocodile Hall could be the stuff of nightmares, but dancing jellyfish, iridescent poison frogs and a real-life 'Nemo' should bring smiles to even the most PlayStation-jaded youngster. (☎030-254 010; www.aquarium-berlin.de; Budapester Strasse 32; adult/child €13/6.50, with zoo €20/10; ⏰9am-6pm; S Zoologischer Garten, 🚇Zoologischer Garten)

Eating

Restaurant am Steinplatz

GERMAN €€€

7 Map p88, D1

The 1920s gets a 21st-century makeover both in the kitchen and the decor at this stylish outpost. The dining room is anchored by an open kitchen where veteran chef Marcus Zimmer uses mostly regional products to execute classic Berlin recipes. Even rustic beer-hall dishes such as *Eisbein* (boiled pork knuckle) are imaginatively reinterpreted and beautifully plated. (☎030-312 6589; www.marriott.de; Hardenbergstrasse 12; mains €16-26; ⏰breakfast, lunch & dinner; 🚌M45, S Ernst-Reuter-Platz, Bahnhof Zoologischer Garten, 🚇Bahnhof Zoologischer Garten)

Local Life

'Little Asia'

If you're in the mood for Asian food simply head to **Kantstrasse** (Map p88, A2-C2) between Savignyplatz and Wilmersdorfer Strasse, which has the city's greatest concentration of Chinese, Vietnamese, Thai and Japanese restaurants, shops and soup kitchens. Most offer value-priced lunches.

Café-Restaurant Wintergarten im Literaturhaus

INTERNATIONAL €€

8 Map p88, D3

The hustle and bustle of Ku'damm is only a block away from this art nouveau villa with attached literary salon and bookstore. Tuck into seasonal bistro cuisine amid elegant Old Berlin flair in the gracefully stucco-ornamented rooms or, if weather permits, in the idyllic garden. Breakfast is served until 2pm. (☎030-882 5414; www.literaturhaus-berlin.de; Fasanenstrasse 23; mains €8-16; ⏰9am-midnight; S Uhlandstrasse)

Neni

INTERNATIONAL €€

The food is actually quite good at this restaurant – located on the same floor as Monkey Bar (see 12 Map p88, G2) – in the 25hours Hotel Bikini Berlin. Enjoy the view while picking from a menu influenced by the cuisines of Israel, Persia, Russia and Arabian and Mediterranean countries. The hummus is reported to be the best in town. (☎030-120 221 200; Budapester Strasse 40; mains €11-21; ⏰noon-10.30pm Sun-Thu, noon-11.30pm Fri & Sat; 🚌100, 200, S Bahnhof Zoologischer Garten, 🚇Bahnhof Zoologischer Garten)

Good Friends

CHINESE €€

9 Map p88, B2

Good Friends is widely considered Berlin's best and most authentic Chinese

Understand

Berlin in the 'Golden' Twenties

The 1920s began as anything but golden, marked by a lost war, social and political instability, hyperinflation, hunger and disease. Many Berliners responded by behaving like there was no tomorrow and made their city as much a den of decadence as a cauldron of creativity. Cabaret, Dada and jazz flourished. Pleasure pits popped up everywhere, turning the city into a 'sextropolis' of Dionysian dimensions. Bursting with energy, it became a laboratory for anything new and modern, drawing giants of architecture (Hans Scharoun, Walter Gropius), fine arts (George Grosz, Max Beckmann) and literature (Bertolt Brecht, Christopher Isherwood).

Cafes & Cabaret

Cabarets provided a titillating fantasy of play and display where transvestites, singers, magicians, dancers and other entertainers made audiences forget the harsh realities. Kurfürstendamm evolved into a major nightlife hub with glamorous cinemas, theatres and restaurants. The Romanisches Café, on the site of today's Europa Center, was practically the second living room for artists, actors, writers, photographers, film producers and other creative types, some famous, most not. German writer Erich Kästner even called it the 'waiting room of the talented'.

Celluloid History

The 1920s and early '30s were also a boom time for Berlin cinema, with Marlene Dietrich seducing the world and the mighty UFA studio producing virtually all of Germany's celluloid output. Fritz Lang, whose seminal works *Metropolis* (1926) and *M* (1931) brought him international fame, was among the dominant filmmakers.

The Crash

The fun came to an instant end when the US stock market crashed in 1929, plunging the world into economic depression. Within weeks, half a million Berliners were jobless, and riots and demonstrations again ruled the streets. The volatile, increasingly polarised political climate led to clashes between communists and the emerging NSDAP (Nazi Party), led by Adolf Hitler. Soon jackboots, Brownshirts, oppression and fear would dominate daily life in Germany.

restaurant. The ducks dangling in the window are the overture to a menu long enough to confuse Confucius. If jellyfish with eggs or fried pork belly prove too challenging, you can always fall back on lemon chicken or king prawn curry. (030-313 2659; www.goodfriends-berlin.de; Kantstrasse 30; mains €7-20; noon-1am; Savignyplatz)

Bier's Kudamm 195

GERMAN €

10 Map p88, B4

This snazzy sausage parlour satisfies the proletarian hunger pangs of deep-pocketed locals, including – if the photographs are anything to go by – the occasional celeb. The truly decadent wash down their *Currywurst* with a small bottle of Champagne (€23). (030-881 8942; Kurfürstendamm 195; Currywurst €2.50; 11am-5am Mon-Thu, 11am-6am Fri & Sat, noon-5pm Sun; U Uhlandstrasse)

Local Life

Berlin's 'Sexy' New Mall

Germany's first concept mall, **Bikini Berlin** (Map88, G2; www.bikiniberlin.de; Budapester Strasse 38-50; 9am-9pm Mon-Sat; S Bahnhof Zoologischer Garten, Bahnhof Zoologischer Garten), opened in 2014 in a spectacularly rehabilitated 1950s architectural icon nicknamed 'Bikini' because of its design: 200m-long upper and lower sections separated by an open floor. It's the domain of urban boutiques stocked with edgy fashion, design, tech gadgets and accessories, many made in Berlin. Even if shopping leaves you cold, come for the industrial-flavoured interior and front-row views of the monkey enclosure of the Berlin Zoo.

Dicke Wirtin

GERMAN €€

11 Map p88, C2

Old Berlin charm oozes from every nook and cranny of this been-here-forever pub which pours eight draught beers (including the superb Kloster Andechs) and nearly three dozen homemade schnapps varieties. Hearty local fare like roast pork, fried liver or breaded schnitzel keeps brains balanced. Bargain lunches. (030-312 4952; www.dicke-wirtin.de; Carmerstrasse 9; mains €6-16; 11am-late; Savignyplatz)

Drinking

Monkey Bar

BAR

12 Map p88, G2

On the 10th floor of the 25hours Hotel Bikini Berlin, this 'urban jungle' hotspot delivers fabulous views of the city and the Berlin Zoo – in summer from a sweeping terrace. Drinks-wise, the list gives prominent nods to tiki concoctions and gin-based cocktail sorcery. The Tiki Reviver, made with apricot brandy and homemade nutmeg syrup, is a signature drink. (030-120 221 210; www.25hours-hotel.com; Budapester Strasse 40; 3pm-1am Mon-Fri, 3pm-2am Sat & Sun; ; 100, 200, S Bahnhof Zoologischer Garten, Bahnhof Zoologischer Garten)

Pearl
CLUB

13 Map p88, E2

This new bauble in Berlin's necklace of party spots has injected some sass into the once fairly sleepy western city centre. Office jockeys invade on Thursdays for the after-work party, Fridays are big with wrinkle-free hip-hop hipsters while dolled-up weekend warriors bust a move beneath the feathery LED light installation on Saturdays. (030-3151 8890; www.thepearl-berlin.com; Fasanenstrasse 81; from 6pm Thu, from 9pm Fri & Sat; M49, S Bahnhof Zoologischer Garten, Bahnhof Zoologischer Garten)

Entertainment

Bar Jeder Vernunft
CABARET

14 Map p88, E5

Life's still a cabaret at this intimate 1912 mirrored tent with playful art nouveau decor, which puts on sophisticated song-and-dance shows, comedy and *chanson* evenings nightly. Seating is in upholstered booths or at little tables. From the U-Bahn station, follow Meierottostrasse for 200m, turn right on Schaperstrasse and continue for another 100m. The entrance is behind the parking lot. (030-883 1582; www.bar-jeder-vernunft.de; Schaperstrasse 24; S Spichernstrasse)

A-Trane
JAZZ

15 Map p88, C1

Herbie Hancock and Diana Krall have anointed the stage of this intimate jazz club, but mostly it's emerging talent bringing their A-game to the A-Trane. Entry is free on Monday when local boy Andreas Schmidt shows off his skills, and after midnight on Saturday for the late-night jam session. (030-313 2550; www.a-trane.de; Bleibtreustrasse 1; 8pm-1am Sun-Thu , 8pm-late Fri & Sat ; Savignyplatz)

Shopping

KaDeWe
DEPARTMENT STORE

16 Map p88, H4

This venerable department store has an assortment so vast that a pirate-style campaign is the best way to plunder its bounty. If pushed for time, at least hurry up to the legendary 6th-floor gourmet food hall. The name, by the way, stands for *Kaufhaus des Westens* (department store of the West). It's right outside U-Bahn station Wittenbergplatz. (030-212 10; www.kadewe.de; Tauentzienstrasse 21-24; 10am-8pm Mon-Thu, 10am-9pm Fri, 9.30am-8pm Sat; S Wittenbergplatz)

Käthe Wohlfahrt
HANDICRAFTS

17 Map p88, E3

With its mind-boggling assortment of traditional German Yuletide decorations, this shop lets you celebrate Christmas year-round. It's accessed via a ramp that spirals around an 8m-high Christmas tree. (www.wohlfahrt.com; Kurfürstendamm 225-226; 10am-7pm Mon-Sat, 1-5pm Sun; S Kurfürstendamm)

Top Sights
Schloss Charlottenburg

Getting There

Schloss Charlottenburg is 3km northwest of Zoologischer Garten.

Ⓤ **U-Bahn** From Sophie-Charlotte-Platz (U2) station it's a scenic 1km walk via Schlossstrasse or a ride on bus 309.

Schloss Charlottenburg is an exquisite baroque palace and one of the few sites in Berlin that still reflects the one-time grandeur of the royal Hohenzollern clan, who ruled from 1415 until 1918. A visit is especially rewarding in summer when you can fold a stroll, sunbathing session or picnic by the carp pond into a day of peeking at royal treasures, including lavishly furnished period rooms and the largest collection of 18th-century French painting outside of France.

Don't Miss

Altes Schloss

The original royal living quarters in the baroque **Old Palace** (⏲10am-6pm Tue-Sun Apr-Oct, 10am-5pm Tue-Sun Nov-Mar) are an extravaganza in stucco, brocade and overall opulence. Admire family portraits in the Oak Gallery, the charming Oval Hall overlooking the park, Chinese and Japanese blueware in the Porcelain Chamber, and the Eosander Chapel with its *trompe l'œil* arches.

Neuer Flügel

Added under Frederick the Great in 1746, the **New Wing** (⏲10am-6pm) contains the palace's most beautiful rooms, including the confection-like White Hall banquet room and the Golden Gallery, a rococo fantasy of mirrors and gilding. Other rooms are filled with paintings by such French masters as Watteau and Pesne.

Schlossgarten

The expansive baroque **gardens** (admission free) linking the palace and the Spree River are part formal French, part unruly English and all idyllic playground. Wandering around the shady paths, lawns and carp pond, you'll eventually stumble upon the sombre Mausoleum and the charming Belvedere.

Belvedere

This pint-size late-rococo **palace** (adult/concession €3/2.50; ⏲10am-6pm Tue-Sun Apr-Oct), built in 1788 as a teahouse for King Friedrich Wilhelm II, today makes an elegant setting for porcelain masterpieces by the royal manufacturer KPM, including lavish dinnerware services.

Neuer Pavillon

This Karl Friedrich Schinkel–designed **mini-palace** (New Pavillion; adult/concession incl audioguide

☎030-320 910

www.spsg.de

Spandauer Damm 10-22

day pass adult/concession €15/11

⏲hours vary by building

🚌M45, 109, 309, S Richard-Wagner-Platz, Sophie Charlotte-Platz

☑ Top Tips

- Arrive early on weekends and in summer to avoid long queues.
- Visit Wednesday to Sunday, when all palace buildings are open.
- The day pass (Charlottenburg+) is valid for admission to all open buildings except the Neuer Flügel.
- A palace visit is easily combined with a spin around the trio of adjacent art museums.

✕ Take a Break

Near the park entrance, the **Kleine Orangerie** (www.kleineorangerie.de; mains €6-15) serves breakfast, snacks, meals and cakes. In fine weather, pack a picnic.

Understand

Palace Planning

Schloss Charlottenburg started out rather modestly as a petite summer palace built for Sophie-Charlotte, wife of Elector Friedrich III (1657–1713). It was expanded in the mode of Versailles after the elector's promotion to king in 1701. Subsequent royals dabbled with the compound, most notably Frederick the Great who added the spectacular Neuer Flügel. The Neuer Pavillon and the Mausoleum and Belvedere in the palace gardens date from the 19th century.

€4/3; ⏰10am-6pm Tue-Sun Apr-Oct, 10am-5pm Nov-Mar) was originally a summer retreat of King Friedrich Wilhelm III (r 1797–1848). Modelled on an Italian villa where the king had stayed, it displays paintings and furniture from the Romantic and Biedermeier periods.

Mausoleum

The neoclassical 1815 **Mausoleum** (adult/concession €2/1; ⏰10am-6pm Tue-Sun Apr-Oct) was conceived as the resting place of the much-beloved Queen Luise but was twice expanded to make room for other royals, including Emperor William I and his wife, Augusta.

Nearby: Sammlung Scharf-Gerstenberg

Surrealist art, including large bodies of work by René Magritte and Max Ernst alongside dreamscapes by Salvador Dalí and Jean Dubuffet, is the ammo of this **museum** (adult/concession €10/5; ⏰10am-6pm Tue-Fri, 11am-6pm Sat & Sun). Standouts among their 18th-century forerunners include Francisco Goya's spooky etchings and the creepy dungeon scenes by Italian engraver Giovanni Battista Piranesi.

Nearby: Bröhan Museum

This fine **museum** (adult/concession/under 18yr €8/5/free; ⏰10am-6pm Tue-Sun) trains the spotlight on art nouveau, art deco and functionalism, decorative styles in vogue between 1889 and 1939. Highlights include period rooms by Hector Guimard and Peter Behrens, a Berlin Secession picture gallery, and a section dedicated to Henry van de Velde.

Nearby: Museum Berggruen

Picasso is especially well represented, with paintings, drawings and sculptures from all his major creative phases, at this delightful **museum** (adult/concession €10/5; ⏰10am-6pm Tue-Fri, 11am-6pm Sat & Sun). Elsewhere it's off to Paul Klee's emotional world, Henri Matisse's paper cut-outs, Alberto Giacometti's skinny sculptures and a sprinkling of African art that inspired them all.

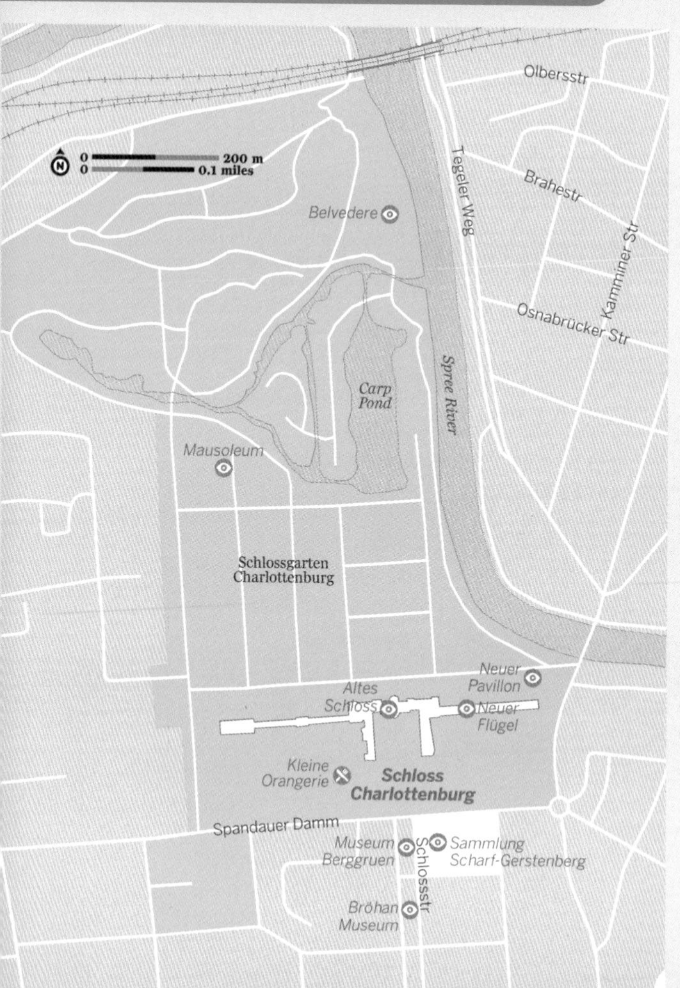
0 200 m
0 0.1 miles
Olbersstr
Brahestr
Tegeler Weg
Kamminer Str
Osnabrücker Str
Belvedere
Carp Pond
Spree River
Mausoleum
Schlossgarten Charlottenburg
Neuer Pavillon
Altes Schloss
Neuer Flügel
Kleine Orangerie
Schloss Charlottenburg
Spandauer Damm
Museum Berggruen
Schlossstr
Sammlung Scharf-Gerstenberg
Bröhan Museum

Local Life
A Leisurely Saunter Through Schöneberg

Getting There

Schöneberg is wedged between Kurfürstendamm and Kreuzberg.

U **U-Bahn** This itinerary is bookended by two stations: Viktoria-Luise-Platz (U4) and Kleistpark (U7).

Schöneberg flaunts a mellow middle-class identity but has a radical pedigree rooted in the squatter days of the '80s. Its multifaceted character nicely unfolds as you stroll from bourgeois Viktoria-Luise-Platz through Berlin's original gay quarter and along streets packed tight with boho cafes and smartly curated indie boutiques, to wind up at ethnically flavoured Hauptstrasse.

Viktoria-Luise-Platz

chöneberg's prettiest square is a ymphony of flower beds, big old trees, lusty fountain and benches where lo-als swap gossip or watch kids at play. 's framed by inviting cafes and 19th-entury townhouses; note the ornate cades at numbers 7, 12 and 12a.

Nollendorfplatz & the Gay Village'

ollendorfplatz has been the gateway Berlin's historic gay quarter since the 920s, when Christopher Isherwood enned *Berlin Stories* (which inspired *abaret*) while living at Nollendorf-rasse 17. Rainbow flags still fly proud- above bars and businesses, especially long Motzstrasse and Fuggerstrasse. A emorial plaque at the U-Bahn station ommemorates Nazi-era GLBT victims.

Farmers Market

it's Wednesday or Saturday morn-g, you're in luck because ho-hum Vinterfeldtplatz erupts with farm-esh fare. Along with seasonal pro-uce you'll find handmade cheeses, ured meats, olives, local honey and enty more staples and surprises. aturday also has artsy-craftsy stalls.

Chocophile Alert

Vinterfeldt Schokoladen (☎030-2362 256; www.winterfeldt-schokoladen.de; oltzstrasse 23; ⏰9am-8pm Mon-Fri, 9am-om Sat, noon-7pm Sun; **S** Nollendorfplatz) ocks a vast range of international andmade gourmet chocolates, all dis-layed gallery-style in the original oak fixtures of a 19th-century pharmacy that doubles as a cafe.

5 Boutique-Hopping

Goltzstrasse and its extension Akazienstrasse teem with indie boutiques selling vintage threads, slinky underwear and handmade jewellery, exotic teas and cooking supplies. No high-street chain in sight! Casual eateries and cafes abound.

6 Double Eye

Javaholics cherish the award-winning espresso of **Double Eye** (Akazienstrasse 22; ⏰9am-6.30pm Mon-Fri, 9am-6pm Sat; **S** Eisenacher Strasse), which is why no one minds the inevitable queue.

7 Möve im Felsenkeller

An artist hang-out since the 1920s, this cosy **pub** (☎030-781 3447; Akazienstrasse 2; ⏰4pm-1am; **S** Eisenacher Strasse) was where Jeffrey Eugenides penned his 2002 Pulitzer Prize winning novel, *Middlesex*. A stuffed seagull dangling from the ceiling keeps an eye on patrons seeking inspiration from eight beers on tap.

8 Hauptstrasse

Chic boutiques give way to grocers and kebab shops along multiculti Hauptstrasse. The Turkish supermarket **Öz-Gida** (www.ozgida.de; Hauptstrasse 16; **S** Kleistpark, Eisenacher Strasse) is known citywide for its olive selection, cheese spreads and quality meats. David Bowie and Iggy Pop shared a pad at Hauptstrasse 155.

Explore

Kreuzberg

Creeping gentrification aside, Kreuzberg is still Berlin's hippest quarter, a bubbly hodgepodge of creatives, students, (life) artists, Turkish-Germans and a global swarm of neo-Berliners. Spend a day searching for street art, soaking up the multiculti vibe, scarfing a shawarma, browsing vintage stores and hanging by the canal, then find out why Kreuzberg is a night-crawler's paradise.

The Sights in a Day

If it's a warm and sunny summer day, there are few better ›laces to start your Kreuzberg sojourn han the **Badeschiff** (p111). Get in a few ours of tanning, swimming and chilling t this riverside beach and swimming ›ool.

Once you've had your relaxation fill, walk north on Schlesische ;trasse, taking in the large-scale **street ırt** of Blu and the unique fashions at **(illerbeast** (p113). For lunch, join the ueue at **Burgermeister** (p109), then ıop on the U1 for the one-stop ride to ;örlitzer Bahnhof (or walk along Skatzer Strasse). Follow Oranienstrasse ıorth, browsing shops like **VooStore** p113) for streetwear, knick-knacks and 'intage fashions. Study the local boho :rowd over coffee (or the first beer of he day) at **Luzia** (p105).

After dark is when Kreuzberg truly comes alive. Dinner opions range from haute cuisine at **Volt** p108) to rib-sticking German classics ıt **Max und Moritz** (p108) or Turkishare at **Defne** (p108). Afterwards you'll ›e ready to launch your dedicated ;tudy of Kreuzberg's bar scene.

'or a local's night in Kreuzberg, see ›104.

Local Life

Kotti Bar-Hop (p104)

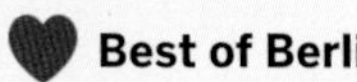

Best of Berlin

Eating

Burgermeister (p109)

Max und Moritz (p108)

Defne (p108)

Bars

Freischwimmer (p110)

Schwarze Traube (p110)

Club der Visionäre (p110)

Clubs

Prince Charles (p111)

Watergate (p111)

Gay & Lesbian

Roses (p105)

Möbel Olfe (p104)

Getting There

Bus A handy line is the M41, which links Kreuzberg with Neukölln, the Hauptbahnhof and Potsdamer Platz.

U-Bahn Getting off at Kottbusser Tor (U8) puts you in the thick of Kreuzberg, but Görlitzer Bahnhof and Schlesisches Tor (both U1) are also good jumping-off points.

Local Life
Kotti Bar-Hop

Noisy, chaotic and sleepless, the area around Kottbusser Tor U-Bahn station (Kotti, for short) defiantly retains the punky-funky alt feel that's defined it since the 1970s. More gritty than pretty, this beehive of snack shops, cafes, pubs and bars delivers some of the city's most hot-stepping night-time action and is tailor-made for dedicated bar-hopping.

1 Funky Salon

A good place to kick the night into gear is **Möbel Olfe** (www.moebel-olfe.de; Reichenberger Strasse 177; ⌚Tue-Sun), an old furniture store recast as an always-busy drinking den with cheap Polish beer and vodka and a friendly crowd that's mixed in every respect (gays dominate on Thursdays, lesbians on Tuesdays). Enter from Dresdener Strasse. Smoking OK.

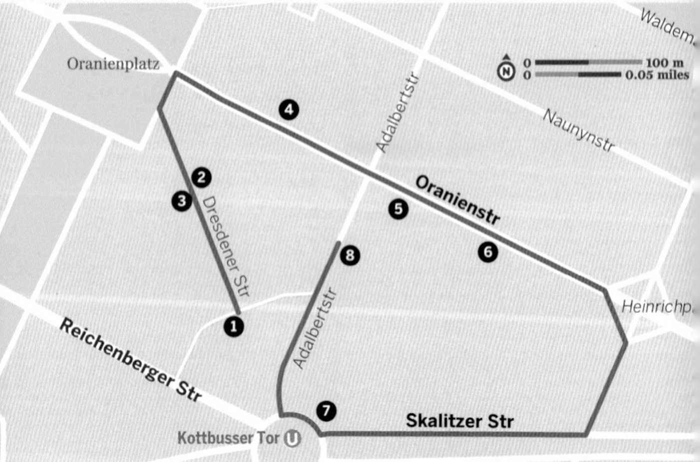

2 Grape Delights

‌Iove on to cosy **Otto Rink** (www.ot-ɔrink.de; Dresdener Strasse 124; ⏲6pm-3am ‌Ion-Sat), a favourite among clued-in ·enophiles. The slate-covered bar ıints at the owner's penchant for vhites from the slate-rich soils of the ‌Iosel region, although other German egions are also well represented, as .re reds from France, Spain and South ımerica.

3 1950s Cocktail Cave

f it's cocktails you're lusting after, ·oint the compass to **Würgeengel** (www.‌uergeengel.de; Dresdener Strasse 122; ⏲from pm), a stylish '50s cocktail cave com-·lete with chandeliers and shiny black ables. It's always buzzy but especially o after the final credits roll at the djacent Babylon cinema.

4 Luscious Lair

'arted up nicely with vintage urniture, baroque wallpaper and vhimsical wall art by Chin Chin, **.uzia** (☎030-8179 9958; Oranienstrasse 4; ⏲from noon till late) draws its crowd rom among more sophisticated local .rban dwellers. It's a trash-stylish spot vith lighting that gives even pasty-aced hipsters a glow.

5 Burlesque Boite

. great place to pull up later in the ıight is **Prinzipal** (☎030-6162 7326; ‌ww.prinzipal-kreuzberg.com; Oranienstrasse 78; ⏲8pm-5am Mon-Sat), an apothecary-tyle burlesque bar that reboots the assy glamour of the 1920s. The menu features all the classics along with 10 signature cocktails named for famous booty-shakers (Date with Dita, Monroe's Kiss etc).

6 Camp of Glam

For contrast, head a few doors down to **Roses** (☎030-615 6570; Oranienstrasse 187; ⏲9pm-late), a kitsch-glittery polysexual pit stop where drinks are cheap and potent. The tiny bar with its pink furry walls gets more packed (and wacky) as the moon gets higher in the sky.

7 MonarchBar

Behind a windowfront at eye level with the elevated U-Bahn tracks, **MonarchBar** (www.kottimonarch.de; Skalitzer Strasse 134; ⏲from 9pm Tue-Sat) is an ingenious blend of trashy sophistication, strong drinks, a relaxed vibe and different DJs nightly playing bouncy electro until the wee hours. Enter via the signless steel door adjacent to the doner kebab shop east of the Kaiser's supermarket.

8 Hasir

An excellent place to restore balance to the brain is **Hasir** (☎030-614 2373; www.hasir.de; Adalbertstrasse 10; mains €8-13; ⏲24hr), the mother branch of a local Turkish mini-chain of restaurants. In the wee hours it's still packed with patrons lusting after grilled meats, stuffed vine leaves and other tasty morsels. Owner Mehmed Aygün claims to have invented the Berlin-style doner kebab back in 1971.

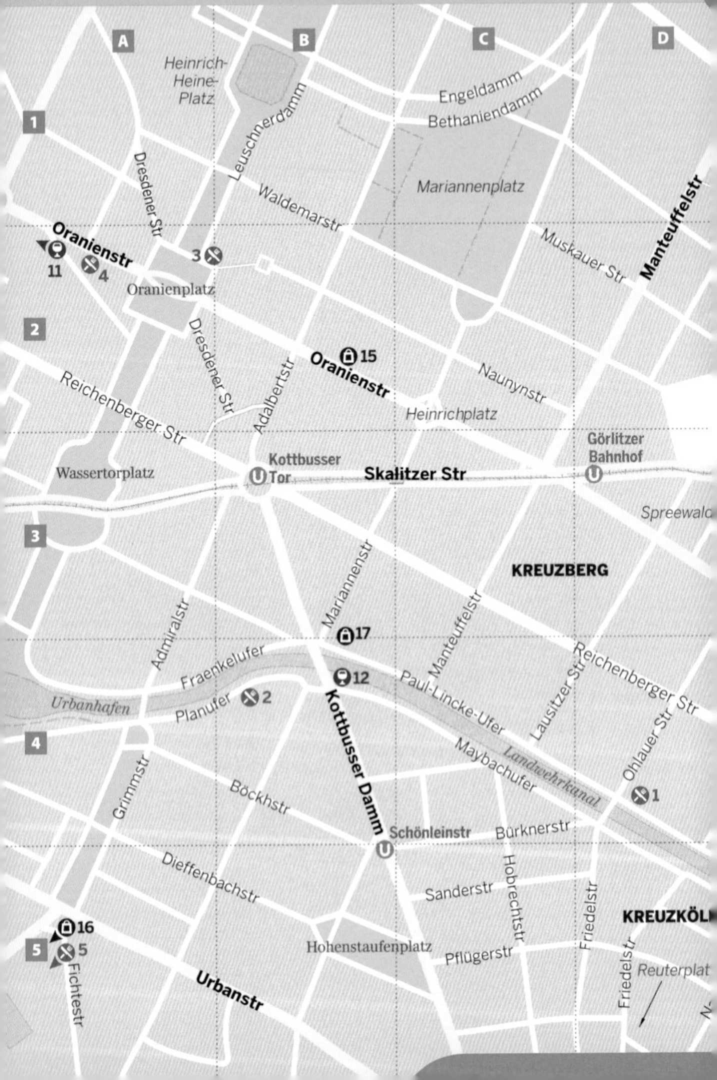

A
B
C
D
1
2
3
4
5
Heinrich-Heine-Platz
Leuschnerdamm
Engeldamm
Bethaniendamm
Mariannenplatz
Dresdener Str
Waldemarstr
Oranienstr
11
4
3
Oranienplatz
Muskauer Str
Manteuffelstr
15
Naunynstr
Heinrichplatz
Adalbertstr
Reichenberger Str
Wassertorplatz
Kottbusser Tor
Skalitzer Str
Görlitzer Bahnhof
Spreewald
KREUZBERG
Mariannenstr
Manteuffelstr
Admiralstr
17
Fraenkelufer
Urbanhafen
Planufer
2
12
Paul-Lincke-Ufer
Lausitzer Str
Reichenberger Str
Ohlauer Str
Maybachufer
Landwehrkanal
1
Grimmstr
Böckhstr
Kottbusser Damm
Schönleinstr
Bürknerstr
Dieffenbachstr
Sanderstr
Hobrechtstr
Friedelstr
16
5
Fichtestr
Hohenstaufenplatz
Pflügerstr
Urbanstr
Reuterplat

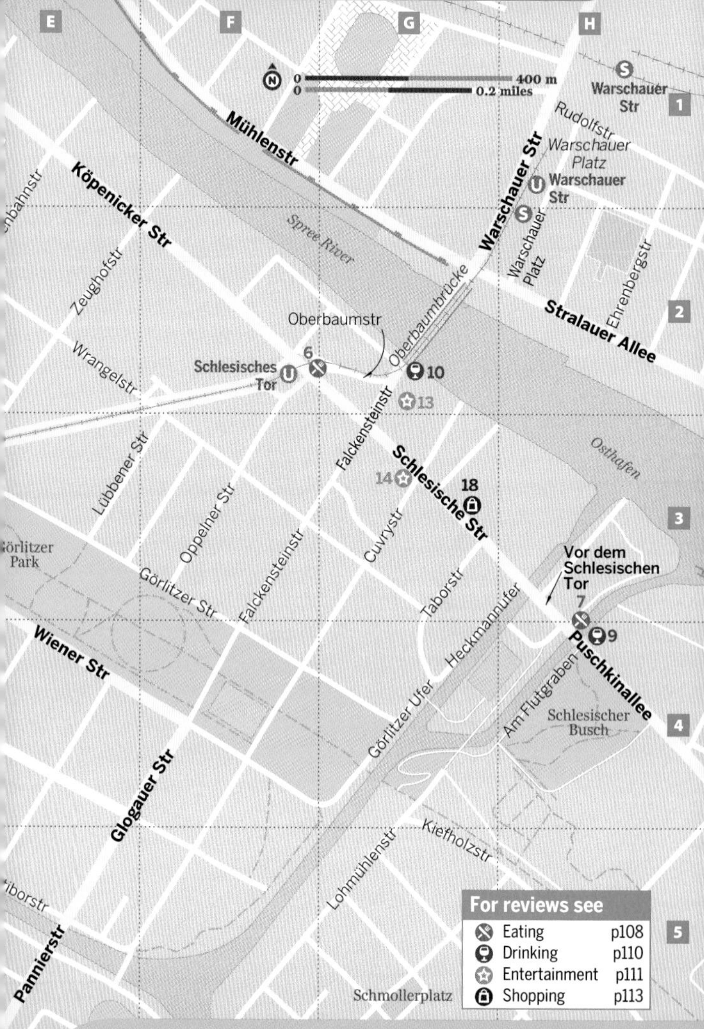

E
F
G
H
1
2
3
4
5
0
400 m
0
0.2 miles
Warschauer Str
Mühlenstr
Köpenicker Str
Rudolfstr
Warschauer Platz
Warschauer Str
Warschauer Str
Warschauer Platz
Spree River
Zeughofstr
Ehrenbergstr
Oberbaumbrücke
Stralauer Allee
Oberbaumstr
Wrangelstr
Schlesisches Tor
6
10
13
Falckensteinstr
Osthafen
Lübbener Str
Schlesische Str
14
18
Oppelner Str
Cuvrystr
Görlitzer Park
Falckensteinstr
Görlitzer Str
Taborstr
Vor dem Schlesischen Tor
7
9
Heckmannufer
Wiener Str
Puschkinallee
Am Flutgraben
Görlitzer Ufer
Schlesischer Busch
Glogauer Str
Kiefholzstr
Lohmühlenstr
Pannierstr
Schmollerplatz
For reviews see
Eating p108
Drinking p110
Entertainment p111
Shopping p113

Eating

Volt

MODERN GERMAN €€€

1 Map p106 D4

The theatrical setting in a 1928 transformer station would be enough to seek out the culinary outpost of Matthias Geiss, crowned Berlin's most promising new chef in 2011. More drama awaits on the plates where smartly combined regional meats, fish and vegetables put on an artful show in innovative yet honest-to-goodness ways. (☎030-338 402 320; www.restaurant-volt.de; Paul-Lincke-Ufer 2; mains €22-32, 4-course dinner €64; ⏰6pm-midnight Mon-Sat; S Görlitzer Bahnhof, Schönleinstrasse)

> Local Life
>
> ### Street Food Thursday
>
> Berlin's most happening foodie event takes over the historic **Markthalle Neun** (Map p106 D2; ☎030-577 094 661; www.markthalleneun.de; Eisenbahnstrasse 42/43; ⏰5-10pm Thu, 10am-6pm Fri & Sat; S Görlitzer Bahnhof) every Thursday from 5pm to 10pm. That's when a changing cast of amateur and semi-pro chefs sets up their food stalls to serve delicious street food from all corners of the world. It's an exotic smorgasbord that might feature New Zealand meat pies, Taiwanese burgers, Argentine pulled pork sandwiches or Korean tacos. Chow down at long communal tables with a glass of wine or a pint of Heidenpeters, a yummy craft beer brewed right on the premises.

Defne

TURKISH €€

2 Map p106, B4

If you thought Turkish cuisine stopped at the doner kebab, canalside Defne will teach you otherwise. The appetiser platter alone elicits intense cravings (fabulous walnut-chilli paste!), but inventive mains such as *ali nacik* (sliced lamb with puréed eggplant and yoghurt) also warrant repeat visits. Lovely summer terrace. (☎030-8179 7111; www.defne-restaurant.de; Planufer 92c; mains €8-20; ⏰4pm-1am Apr-Sep, 5pm-1am Oct- Mar; S Kottbusser Tor, Schönleinstrasse)

Henne

GERMAN €€

3 Map p106 A2

This Old Berlin institution operates on the KISS (keep it simple, stupid!) principle: milk-fed chicken spun on the rotisserie for moist yet crispy perfection. That's all it's been serving for over a century, alongside tangy potato and white cabbage salads. Eat in the garden or in the cosy 1907 dining room that's resisted the tides of time. Reservations essential. (☎030-614 7730; www.henne-berlin.de; Leuschnerdamm 25; half chicken €7.90; ⏰6pm-midnight Tue-Sat, 5pm-midnight Sun; S Moritzplatz)

Max und Moritz

GERMAN €€

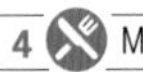
4 Map p106, A2

The patina of yesteryear hangs over this ode-to-old-school brewpub named for the cheeky Wilhelm Busch cartoon characters. Since 1902 it has packed

Currywurst, Curry 36

hungry diners and drinkers into its rustic tile-and-stucco ornamented rooms for sudsy home brews and granny-style Berlin fare. A menu favourite is the *Kutschergulasch* (goulash cooked with beer). (☎030-6951 5911; www.maxundmoritzberlin.de; Oranienstrasse 162; mains €9.50-17; ⏲5pm-midnight; S Moritzplatz)

Curry 36

GERMAN €

5 Map p106, A5

Day after day, night after night, a motley crowd – cops, cabbies, queens, office jockeys, savvy tourists etc – wait their turn at this top-ranked Currywurst purveyor that's been frying 'em up since 1981. (☎030-251 7368; www.curry36.de; Mehringdamm 36; snacks €2-6; ⏲9am-5am; S Mehringdamm)

Burgermeister

AMERICAN €

6 Map p106, F2

It's green, ornate, a century old and... it used to be a toilet. Now it's a burger joint beneath the elevated U-Bahn tracks. Don't fret, don't shudder: the plump all-beef patties are tops (try the Meisterburger with fried onions, bacon and barbecue sauce) and great with fries and homemade dips such as peanut and mango curry. (www.burgermeister.de; Oberbaumstrasse 8; burgers €3-4.50; ⏲11am-3am Sun-Thu, to 4am Fri & Sat; S Schlesisches Tor)

Freischwimmer
CAFE €€

7 Map p106, H3

In summertime, few places are more idyllic than this rustic 1930s boathouse turned canalside chill zone. The kitchen has of late stepped up its game and now offers meat and fish cooked to perfection on a lava rock grill, in addition to crisp salads and *Flammekuche* (Alsatian pizza). It's also a popular Sunday brunch spot. Kayak and boat rentals available. (030-6107 4309; www.freischwimmer-berlin.de; Vor dem Schlesischen Tor 2a; mains €8-17; from noon Mon-Fri, from 10am Sat & Sun; S Schlesisches Tor)

Drinking

Schwarze Traube
BAR

8 Map p106, E2

Mixologist Atalay Aktas was Germany's Best Bartender of 2013 and this pint-sized drinking parlour is where he and his staff create their magic potions. Since there's no menu, each drink is calibrated to the taste and mood of each patron using premium spirits, expertise and a dash of psychology. (030-2313 5569; www.facebook.com/schwarzetraube1; Wrangelstrasse 24; 7pm-5am; S Görlitzer Bahnhof)

Club der Visionäre
CLUB

9 Map p106, H4

It's cold beer, crispy pizza and fine electro at this summertime chill and party playground in an old canalside boatshed. Park yourself beneath the weeping willows, stake out some turf on the upstairs deck or hit the teensy dance floor. At weekends party people invade. The toilets suck. (030-6951 8942; www.clubdervisionaere.com; Am Flutgraben 1; from 2pm Mon-Fri, from noon Sat & Sun; S Schlesisches Tor, R Treptower Park)

Understand

Street Art

Berlin is sometimes called the world's street art capital and, indeed, some of the hottest players have left their mark on local walls: international artists Blu, JR and Os Gemeos sit alongside local talent like Bonk, Bimer and El Bocho. In the vicinity of U-Bahn station Schlesisches Tor are some house-wall-size classics, for instance *Leviathan* by Blu (next to Watergate) and *Yellow Man* by the Brazilian twins Os Gemeos on Oppelner Strasse. Skalitzer Strasse is also a fertile hunting ground, with Victor Ash's *Astronaut* and ROA's *Nature Morte* being highlights. Keep your eyes open, check out the blog of **Street Art Berlin** (www.streetart-bln.com) or join a guided tour, such as those by **Alternative Berlin Tours** (0162 819 8264; www.alternativeberlin.com) .

Watergate

CLUB

10 Map p106, G2

For a short night's journey into day, check into this high-octane riverside club with two floors, panoramic windows and a floating terrace overlooking the Oberbaumbrücke and Universal Music. Top DJs keep electro-hungry hipsters hot and sweaty till way past sunrise. Long queues, tight door. (030-6128 0394; www.water-gate.de; Falckensteinstrasse 49a; from midnight Wed, Fri & Sat; S Schlesisches Tor)

Prince Charles

CLUB

11 Map p106, A2

Prince Charles is a stylish mix of club and bar ensconced in a former pool and overlooked by a kitschy-cute fish mural. Electro, techno and house rule the turntables on weekends. The venue also hosts concerts, gay parties and the 'Burgers & Hip Hop' street food party. In summer, the action spills into the courtyard. (030-200 950 933; www.princecharlesberlin.com; Prinzenstrasse 85f; from 7pm Wed-Sat; S Moritzplatz)

Ankerklause

PUB

12 Map p106, B4

Ahoy there! This nautical kitsch tavern with an arse-kicking jukebox sets sail in an old harbour-master's shack; it's great for quaffing and waving to the boats puttering along the canal. Breakfast, burgers and snacks provide sustenance. (030-693 5649; www.ankerklause.de; Kottbusser Damm 104; from 4pm Mon, from 10am Tue-Sun; S Schönleinstrasse)

Local Life

All Aboard the Badeschiff

Take an old river barge, fill with water, moor in the Spree River and voila: the **Badeschiff** (Map p106, H3; 030-533 2030; www.arena-berlin.de; Eichenstrasse 4; summer adult/concession €5/3; 8am-midnight May-Sep, shorter hours in winter; 265, S Schlesische Strasse, Treptower Park), the preferred swim-and-tan spot for Berlin kool kids. After-dark action includes parties, bands, movies and simply hanging out. In winter it's all covered up and turned into a deliciously toasty chill zone with saunas and lounge bar.

Entertainment

Magnet Club

LIVE MUSIC

13 Map p106, G2

This indie and alt-sound bastion is known for bookers with an astronomer's ability to detect stars in the making. After the last riff, the mostly student-age crowd hits the dance floor to – depending on the night – Britpop, indietronics, neodisco, rock or punk. (www.magnet-club.de; Falckensteinstrasse 48; S Schlesisches Tor)

Understand

Berlin's Milestones in Music

Since the end of WWII, Berlin has spearheaded most of Germany's popular music innovations. In the late 1960s, Tangerine Dream helped propagate the psychedelic sound while a decade later Kreuzberg's subculture launched the punk movement at SO36 and other famous clubs. Inspired by Berlin's brooding mood, David Bowie and Iggy Pop lived in Schöneberg in the late 1970s, a period that saw Bowie record his Berlin Trilogy (*Low, Heroes, Lodger*) at the famous Hansa Studios.

Punk diva Nina Hagen, meanwhile, helped chart the course for Neue Deutsche Welle (NDW; German new wave) in the early 1980s, which produced such local bands as D.A.F, Neonbabies and Ideal. The '80s also saw the birth of the still-popular punk rock band Die Ärzte, and Einstürzende Neubauten who pioneered a proto-industrial sound that transformed oil drums, electric drills and chainsaws into musical instruments. Its founder Blixa Bargeld became a guitarist and vocalist with Nick Cave & the Bad Seeds. The small but vital East Berlin punk scene produced Sandow and Feeling B, members of whom went on to form the industrial metal band Rammstein in 1994, which is still Germany's top musical export.

Since the 1990s, electronic beats have shaped the Berlin sound, spawned a near-mythical club culture and, to no small degree, defined the capital's cool factor and put it on the map of global hedonists. What today is a huge industry germinated in a dark and dank cellar club called UFO back in 1988 where the scene's 'godfathers' – Dr Motte, Westbam and Kid Paul – played their first gigs. It was Motte who came up with the bright idea to take the party to the street with a truck, loud beats and a bunch of friends dancing behind it – thus, the Love Parade was born (it peaked in 1999 with dozens of trucks and 1.5 million ravers swarming Berlin's streets). *The Beauty of Transgression: A Berlin Memoir,* by US-born artist (and partner of Einstürzende Neubauten bassist Andreas Hacke) Danielle de Picciotto, beautifully captures the atmosphere and history of Berlin's creative underground from the 1980s to today.

Lido
LIVE MUSIC

14 Map p106, G3

A 1950s cinema has been recycled into a rock-indie-electro-pop mecca with mosh-pit electricity and a crowd that cares more about the music than about looking good. Global DJs and talented upwardly mobile live noise-makers pull in the punters. Holds legendary Balkanbeats parties every few weeks. (030-6956 6840; www.lido-berlin.de; Cuvrystrasse 7; S Schlesisches Tor)

Shopping

VooStore
FASHION, ACCESSORIES

15 Map p106, B2

Kreuzberg's first concept store opened in an old backyard locksmith shop off gritty Oranienstrasse, stocking style-forward designer threads and accessories by such crave-worthy labels as Acne, Soulland, Kenzo and Carven and dozens more along with tightly curated books, gadgets, mags and spirits. (030-6165 1119; www.vooberlin.com; Oranienstrasse 24; 11am-8pm Mon-Sat; S Kottbusser Tor)

Another Country
BOOKS

16 Map p106, A5

Run by the eccentric Sophie Raphaeline, this nonprofit boho outfit is really more a library and (counter-cultural) salon than a bookshop. Pick a tome from around 20,000 used English-language books – classic lit to science fiction – and, if you want, sell it back, minus a €1.50 borrowing fee. Also hosts an English Filmclub (9pm Tuesday) and dinners (8pm Friday). (030-6940 1160; www.anothercountry.de; Riemannstrasse 7; 2-8pm Mon, 11am-8pm Tue-Fri, noon-6pm Sat; S Gneisenaustrasse)

Hard Wax
MUSIC

17 Map p106, B3

This well-hidden outpost has been on the cutting edge of electronic music for about two decades and is a must-stop for fans of techno, house, minimal, dubstep and whatever permutation comes along next. (030-6113 0111; www.hardwax.com; Paul-Lincke-Ufer 44a, 3rd fl, door A, 2nd courtyard; noon-8pm Mon-Sat; S Kottbusser Tor)

Killerbeast
FASHION

18 Map p106, G3

'Kill uniformity' is the motto of this boutique where Claudia and her colleagues have made new clothes from old ones long before 'upcycling' entered the urban dictionary. No two pieces are alike and prices are very reasonable. There's even a line for kids. (030-9926 0319; www.killerbeast.de; Schlesische Strasse 31; 3-8pm Mon, 1-8pm Tue-Fri, 1-5pm Sat; S Schlesisches Tor)

Local Life
Nosing Around Neukölln

Getting There

Neukölln is just south of Kreuzberg, separated from it by the Landwehrkanal.

U U-Bahn Start at Schönleinstrasse (U8). The closest stop to the finish line is Boddinstrasse (U8).

South of Kreuzberg, northern Neukölln knows what it's like to go from troubled neighbourhood to hipster haven. For decades the area made headlines, mostly for its high crime rate and poor schools, only to get 'discovered' a few years ago by a cash-poor and idea-rich international crowd. Today the 'hood flaunts a thriving DIY ethos and teems with funky bars, galleries, project spaces and cafes, most of them run by an international cast of creative neo-Berliners.

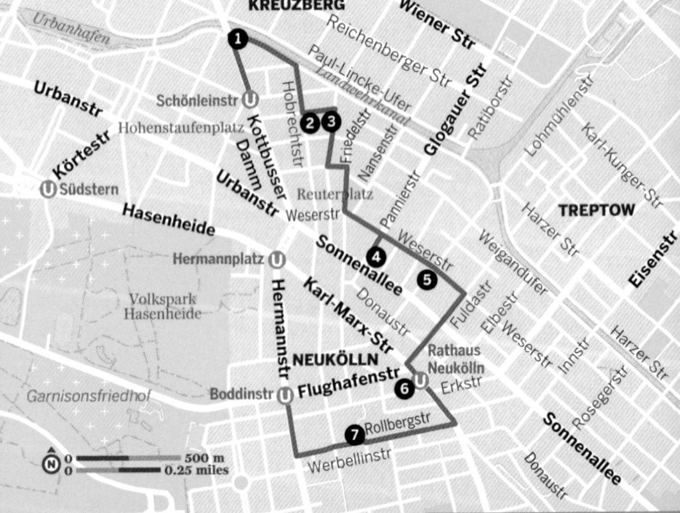

1 Canalside Marketeering

Start by walking a short stretch of the Maybachufer, a scenic section of the Landwehrkanal. The best time to visit is Tuesday or Friday afternoons when the **Türkenmarkt** (Turkish farmer's market; www.tuerkenmarkt.de; S Schönleinstrasse, Kottbusser Tor) is in full swing. Join hipsters in their quest for exotic cheese spreads, crusty flatbreads and mountains of produce. In the warmer months, a fun flea and local designer market called **Nowkoelln Flowmarkt** (www.nowkoelln.de; 10am-6pm 2nd & 4th Sun of month) takes over the river bank.

2 CafeShop

Is it a store? Or a cafe? In fact, **Sing Blackbird** (030-5484 5051; Sanderstrasse 11; noon-7pm Mon-Sat; ; S Schönleinstrasse) sings its song for lovers of vintage clothing *and* fabulous homemade cakes and locally roasted java. Browse racks of threads from the '70s to the '90s, then revel in your purchases over a steamy cuppa.

3 Frosty Delights

Neighbourhood-adored **Fräulein Frost's** (Friedelstrasse 39; from 1pm Mon-Fri, from noon Sat & Sun; S Schönleinstrasse) ice-cream parlour is all about experimentation, as reflected in such courageous concoctions as the bestselling GuZiMi, which stands for Gurke-Zitrone-Minze (cucumber-lemon-mint).

4 Burger Bonanza

The guys at **Berlin Burger International** (0178 540 7409; www.berlinburger-international.com; Pannierstrasse 5; burgers €4.90-7.50; noon-midnight Mon-Thu, to 1am Fri, to 10pm Sun; ; S Hermannplatz) know that size matters, at least when it comes to burgers: handmade, two-fisted contenders.

5 Weserstrasse

This is the main drag to feed your party animal, with an eclectic mix of pubs and bars: take your pick from clubbing at **Fuchs & Elster** (www.fuchsundelster.com; Weserstrasse 207; M41, M29, S Hermannplatz), wine at **Vin Aqua Vin** (030-9405 2886; www.vinaquavin.de; Weserstrasse 204; from 3pm), vamping at campy **Silverfuture** (030-7563 4987; www.silverfuture.net; Weserstrasse 206; 5pm-2am Sun-Thu, to 3am Fri & Sat) or a cocktail at **Das TiER** (Weserstrasse 42; 7pm-2am).

6 Rooftop Partying

In the warmer months, the club-garden-beach-bar combo called **Klunkerkranich** (www.klunkerkranich.de; Karl-Marx-Strasse 66; 10am-midnight Mon-Sat, noon-midnight Sun, weather permitting; S Rathaus Neukölln), on the rooftop of the Neukölln Arcaden shopping mall, invites chilling with a view.

7 Brewery Reborn

The sprawling 1920s Kindl brewery has been reincarnated as an art complex anchored by the **Kindl Centre for Contemporary Art** (www.kindl-berlin.com; Am Sudhaus 2; S Boddinstrasse, Rathaus Neukölln), which started presenting exhibits in autumn 2014. A co-tenant is queer party institution **SchwuZ** (030-5770 2270; www.schwuz.de; Rollbergstrasse 26; Wed-Sun; 104,167, S Rathaus Neukölln).

Explore

Friedrichshain

Rents may be rising and gentrification unstoppable, but for now there's still plenty of partying to be done in this student-heavy district. Soak up the socialist vibe on Karl-Marx-Allee and revel in post-reunification euphoria at the East Side Gallery before finding your favourite libation station(s) around Boxhagener Platz or along Revaler Strasse and capping the night with a dedicated dance a thon in a top electro club.

The Sights in a Day

Make your way to Ostbahnhof and confront the ghosts of the Cold War on a stroll along the **East Side Gallery** (p118). After giving your camera a workout, either pop into the cafe at **Universal Music** (p119) for a late-morning pick-me-up or report straight to **Michelberger** (p119) for lunch.

Walk over to **Karl-Marx-Allee** (p122), East Berlin's showcase boulevard, to parade alongside the phalanx of monumental buildings, some clad in Meissen tiles. Drop by **Café Sibylle** (p124) to learn more about the street's history and architecture before hopping on the U5 at Strausberger Platz to ride the three stops to Samariterstrasse. Head towards Boxhagener Platz for an aimless wander, poking into boho boutiques and watching the world on parade from one of the many cafes.

Reflect upon the day's events over locally brewed pilsner at **Hops & Barley** (p123), then waltz over to **Lemon Leaf** (p123) for an Asian dinner or **Lisboa Bar** (p123) for Portuguese. Wrap up the evening over cocktails at **Chapel Bar** (p124) or find your fave from among the clubs and bars on the **RAW Gelände** (p123) along Revaler Strasse.

Top Sights

East Side Gallery (p118)

Best of Berlin

Clubs

Berghain/Panorama Bar (p124)

://about blank (p124)

Suicide Circus (p124)

Music & Performance

Astra Kulturhaus (p125)

Gay & Lesbian

Berghain/Panorama Bar (p124)

Himmelreich (p125)

Monster Ronson's Ichiban Karaoke (p125)

Getting There

S **S-Bahn** Warschauer Strasse and Ostkreuz (S3, S5, S7/75, S9) are both handy stops.

Tram The M13 goes from Warschauer Strasse station to Boxhagener Platz.

U **U-Bahn** Frankfurter Tor (U5) and Warschauer Strasse (U1) are your best bets.

Top Sights
East Side Gallery

The year was 1989. After 28 years, the Berlin Wall, that grim divider of humanity, finally met its maker. Most of it was quickly dismantled, but along Mühlenstrasse, paralleling the Spree River, a 1.3km stretch became the East Side Gallery, the world's largest open-air mural collection. In more than 100 paintings, dozens of international artists translated the era's global euphoria and optimism into a mix of political statements, drug-induced musings and truly artistic visions.

Map p120, C4

www.eastsidegallery-berlin.de

Mühlenstrasse btwn Oberbaumbrücke & Ostbahnhof

admission free

S Warschauer Strasse, Ostbahnhof, Warschauer Strasse

Mural by César Olhagaray

Don't Miss

Dimitry Vrubel: My God, Help Me Survive amid This Deadly Love

The gallery's best-known painting, showing Soviet and GDR leaders Leonid Brezhnev and Erich Honecker locking lips with eyes closed, is based on an actual photograph taken by French journalist Regis Bossu during Brezhnev's 1979 Berlin visit. This kind of kiss was an expression of great respect in socialist countries.

Birgit Kinder: Test the Rest

Another shutterbug favourite is Birgit Kinder's painting of a GDR-era Trabant car (known as a Trabi) bursting through the Wall with the licence plate reading 'NOV•9–89', the day the barrier was shattered.

Kani Alavi: It Happened in November

A wave of people squeezes through a breached Wall in a metaphorical rebirth in Kani Alavi's recollection of the events of 9 November. Note the different facial expressions, ranging from hope, joy and euphoria to disbelief and fear.

Thierry Noir: Homage to the Young Generation

French artist Thierry Noir's boldly coloured cartoon-like heads symbolise the new-found freedom after the Wall's collapse.

Thomas Klingenstein: Detour to the Japanese Sector

Born in East Berlin, Thomas Klingenstein spent time in a Stasi prison for dissent before being extradited to West Germany in 1980. This mural was inspired by his childhood love for Japan, where he ended up living from 1984 to the mid-'90s.

☑ Top Tips

▶ The more-famous paintings are near the Ostbahnhof end, so start your walk here if you've got limited time.

▶ For more street art, check out the river-facing side of the Wall.

✕ Take a Break

The hipster hotel **Michelberger** (Map p120, D4; Warschauer Strasse 39-40; mains €5-10; ⌚lunch Mon-Fri; 📶; S Warschauer Strasse, U Warschauer Strasse) serves excellent all-organic breakfasts and lunches.

Mingle with media types for coffee, snacks or a hot lunch in the riverside cafe of **Universal Music** (Map p120, D5; Stralauer Allee 1; ⌚8am-8pm Mon-Fri Apr-Sep, 8am-6pm Mon-Fri Oct-Mar).

A B C D

1 2 3 4 5

Strausberger Platz
Weidenweg
Weberwiese
Karl-Marx-Al
Krautstr
Strasse der Pariser Kommune
Singerstr
Koppenstr
Franz-Mehring-Platz
Marchlewskistr
Gubener Str
Andreasstr
Rüdersdorfer Str
Wedekindstr
Wriezener Karree
Corneliusplatz
Ostbahnhof 15
8
Ostbahnhof
Am Ostbahnhof
Stralauer Platz
An der Ostbahn
Helsingforser Str
Schillingbrücke
FRIEDRICHSHAIN
Mühlenstr
Helen-Ernst-Str
Helsingfors Pla
Mildred-Harnack-Str
O2 World
Hedwig-Wachenheim-Str
Tamara-Danz-Str
East Side Gallery
12
0 400 m
0 0.2 miles
Warschauer Str
Manteuffelstr
Warschauer Platz
Spree River
Köpenicker Str
Am Oberbaum
Stralauer Al
Schlesisches Tor
Oberbaumbrücke

For reviews see

Top Sights	p118
Sights	p122
Eating	p122
Drinking	p123
Entertainment	p125
Shopping	p125

E
F
G
H
1
2
3
4
5
Bänschstr
Rigaer Str
Proskauer Str
Schreinerstr
Samariterstr
Frankfurter Tor
1
Karl-Marx-Allee
Frankfurter Allee
Samariterstr
Niederbarnimstr
Mainzer Str
Weichselstr
Boxhagener Str
Grünberger Str
Simon-Dach-Str
4
Gabriel-Max-Str
Gärtnerstr
14
Boxhagener Platz
Kopernikusstr
11
5
Krossener Str
Holteistr
Warschauer Str
3
Wühlischstr
6
Simplonstr
Seumestr
13
Revaler Str
Sonntagstr
Warschauer
7
Lenbachstr
Neue Bahnhofstr
Rudolfstr
Rotherstr
Rudolfplatz
Modersohnstr
Ostkreuz
Hauptstr
Corinthstr
10

Sights

Karl-Marx-Allee

STREET

1 Map p120, E1

It's easy to feel like Gulliver in the Land of Brobdingnag when walking down monumental Karl-Marx-Allee, one of Berlin's most impressive GDR-era relics. Built between 1952 and 1960, the 90m-wide boulevard runs for 2.3km between Alexanderplatz and Frankfurter Tor and is a fabulous showcase of East German architecture. A considerable source of national pride back then, it provided modern flats for comrades and served as a backdrop for military parades. (S Strausberger Platz, Weberwiese, Frankfurter Tor)

Eating

Mio Matto

VEGAN €€€

2 Map p120, D4

Chandeliers meet red-and-white-checkered tablecloths. And vegan meets Italian on the menu. At his new outpost, Björn Moschinkski likes to orchestrate opposites, often making plate-fellows out of surprising ingredients, usually with great success. The well-stocked bar, weekend brunch and daily lunch specials have their devotees. (030-364 281 040; www.miomatto.de; Warschauer Strasse 33; mains €15-19, 3-/4-course dinner from €23/27; noon-10pm; ; S Warschauer Strasse, M10, U Warschauer Strasse)

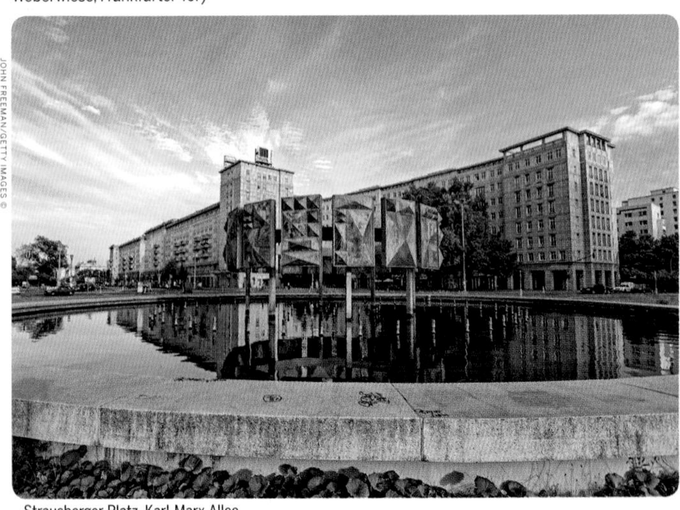

Strausberger Platz, Karl-Marx-Allee

Spätzle & Knödel

GERMAN €€

3  Map p120, G3

This elbows-on-the-table gastropub is a great place to get your southern German comfort food fix, from waist-expanding portions of roast pork, goulash and of course the eponymous *Spätzle* (German mac 'n' cheese) and *Knödel* (dumplings). Check the blackboard for seasonal specials like venison goulash or wild boar stew. Bonus: Bavarian Riegele, Maisel and Weihenstephan beers on tap. (☎030-2757 1151; www.spaetzleknoedel.de; Wühlischstrasse 20; mains €7-14; ⌚5-11pm; S Samariterstrasse)

Lemon Leaf

ASIAN €

4  Map p120, F3

Cheap and cheerful, this place is always swarmed by loyal local hipsters and for good reason: light, inventive and fresh, the Vietnamese menu has few false notes. Intriguing choice: the sweet-sour Indochine Salad with banana blossoms. (☎030-2900 9428; www.lemonleaf.de; Grünberger Strasse 69; mains €6-9; ⌚noon-midnight; ✍; S Frankfurter Tor)

Lisboa Bar

PORTUGUESE €€

5  Map p120, F3

Thanks to an expansion, getting a table at this beloved Portuguese outpost is no longer as tall an order. The hearty tapas are an excellent base for a dedicated neighbourhood pub crawl. Try the *pasteis de bacalhau* (fish dumplings), brandy shrimp or chicken in hot piri-piri sauce or any of the weekly specials. (☎030-9362 1978; www.lisboa-bar-berlin.de; Krossener Strasse 20; tapas €3-10; ⌚from 5pm Mon, from 3pm Tue-Fri, from 11am Sat & Sun; S Warschauer Strasse, Samariterstrasse, M13, Warschauer Strasse)

Local Life

Urban Playground

The postindustrial jumble of derelict buildings along Revaler Strasse, called **RAW Gelände** (Map p120, E4; along Revaler Strasse; S Warschauer Strasse, Warschauer Strasse, Ostkreuz), is one of the last alternative compounds in central Berlin. Since 1999 these rambling, graffiti-slathered grounds of a 19th-century train repair station have been a thriving offbeat creative centre dotted with clubs and bars, an indoor skate park and – in summer – a bunker-turned-climbing-wall with attached beer garden and outdoor cinema. Flea market and street food-fair on Sundays.

Drinking

Hops & Barley

PUB

6 Map p120, G3

Conversation flows as freely as the unfiltered pilsner, malty *Dunkel* (dark), fruity *Weizen* (wheat) and potent cider produced at this congenial microbrewery inside a former butcher's shop. For variety, the brewmeisters produce seasonal blackboard specials such as a malty Bernstein or a robust Indian Pale Ale. (☎030-2936 7534; Wühlischstrasse 40;

Top Tip

Spotlight on KMA

For more background on the Karl-Marx-Allee (KMA), drop by **Café Sybille** (Map p120, B1; ☎030-2935 2203; www.cafe-sibylle-berlin.de; Karl-Marx-Allee 72; exhibit free, rooftop 1-5 people €15, extra person €3; ⏰10am-8pm Mon-Wed, 10am-10pm Thu & Fri, noon-10pm Sat & Sun, rooftop 1-5pm Mon, Wed & Fri; S Weberwiese, Strausberger Platz), which has coffee, a small exhibit charting the milestones of the boulevard from inception to today, and Instagram-worthy views of the boulevard from the rooftop.

⏰from 5pm Mon-Fri, from 3pm Sat & Sun; S Warschauer Strasse, Warschauer Strasse)

Chapel Bar

COCKTAIL BAR

7 Map p120, G4

Another star on the Friedrichshain cocktail firmament is the Chapel Bar. Its 'altar' is helmed by meister mixer Michael Blair, whose repertory includes both classic and out-there drinks like the Jägermeister-based Hubertus & Jade. A giant chandelier bathes the otherwise rather simple room in a complexion-friendly glow. (☎030-6593 6574; www.chapelberlin.com; Sonntagstrasse 30; ⏰from 6pm; Ostkreuz)

Berghain/Panorama Bar

CLUB

8 Map p120, C3

Only world-class spinmasters heat up this hedonistic bass junkie hellhole inside a labyrinthine ex-power plant. Hard-edged minimal techno dominates the ex-turbine hall (Berghain) while house dominates at Panorama Bar one floor up. Strict door, no cameras. Check the website for midweek concerts and record-release parties at the main venue and the adjacent **Kantine am Berghain** (☎030-2936 0210; www.berghain.de; Am Wriezener Bahnhof; ⏰hrs vary; Ostbahnhof).

Suicide Circus

CLUB

9 Map p120, E4

Tousled hipsters hungry for an eclectic electro shower invade this gritty dancing den that at times can feel like a mini-Berghain – sweaty, edgy, industrial and with a top-notch sound system. In summer, watch the stars fade on the outdoor floor with chillier sounds and grilled bratwurst. (www.suicide-berlin.com; Revaler Strasse 99; ⏰usually Wed-Sun; Warschauer Strasse)

://about blank

CLUB

10 Map p120, G5

This club collective also organises cultural and political events that often segue into long, intense club nights, when talented DJs feed a diverse bunch of revellers dance-worthy electronic gruel. Drinks are fairly priced, and if you get the spirit of openness and tolerance, you'll have a grand old time. (www.aboutparty.net; Markgrafendamm 24c; ⏰Fri & Sat; Ostkreuz)

Himmelreich GAY

11 Map p120, F3

Confirming all those stereotypes about gays having good taste, this smart red-hued cocktail bar cum retro-style lounge makes most of the competition look like a straight guy's bedsit. Tuesdays are women-only and on Wednesdays drinks are two-for-one. (030-2936 9292; www.himmelreich-berlin.de; Simon-Dach-Strasse 36; 6pm-2am Mon-Thu, 6pm-4am Fri, 2pm-4am Sat, 2pm-2am Sun; S Warschauer Strasse, Warschauer Strasse)

Monster Ronson's Ichiban Karaoke KARAOKE

12 Map p120, D4

Knock back a couple of brewskis if you need to loosen your nerves before belting out your best Beyonce or Lady Gaga at this mad, great karaoke joint. *Pop Idol* wannabes too shy to hit the stage can book a booth for music and mischief in private. Some nights are GLBT-geared, like Mondays' Multi-SEXxual BOXhopping. Must be 21 to enter. (030-8975 1327; www.karaokemonster.com; Warschauer Strasse 34; from 7pm; S Warschauer Strasse, Warschauer Strasse)

Entertainment

Astra Kulturhaus LIVE MUSIC

13 Map p120, E4

With space for 1500, Astra is one of the bigger indie venues in town, yet often fills up easily, and not just for such headliners as Melissa Etheridge, Kasabian or Paul van Dyk's Vandit Records label parties. Bonus: the sweet '50s GDR decor. Beer garden in summer. (030-2005 6767; www.astra-berlin.de; Revaler Strasse 99; S Warschauer Strasse, Warschauer Strasse)

Shopping

Flohmarkt am Boxhagener Platz FLEA MARKET

14 Map p120, F3

Wrapping around leafy Boxhagener Platz, this fun flea market is just a java whiff away from Sunday brunch cafes. Among vendors it's easy to sniff out the pros from the regular folks here to unload their spring-cleaning detritus for pennies. (Boxhagener Platz; 10am-6pm Sun; S Warschauer Strasse, Frankfurter Tor, Warschauer Strasse)

Antikmarkt am Ostbahnhof FLEA MARKET, ANTIQUES

15 Map p120, B3

There are two sections to this market which starts outside the station's north exit. The 'Grosser Antikmarkt' (large antiques market) is more professional and brims with such genuine collectibles as old coins, Iron Curtain–era relics, gramophone records, books, stamps and jewellery. It segues neatly into the 'Kleiner Antikmarkt' (small antiques market) which has more bric-a-brac and lower prices. (www.oldthing.de; Erich-Steinfurth-Strasse; 9am-5pm Sun; Ostbahnhof)

Explore

Prenzlauer Berg

Prenzlauer Berg went from rags to riches after reunification, to emerge as one of Berlin's most desirable neighbourhoods. There are no must-sees, just ample local charms that reveal themselves on a leisurely meander. Look up at restored townhouses, comb side streets for indie boutiques or carve out a spot in a charismatic cafe. On Sundays, the Mauerpark is a heaving haven of fun, flea-market browsing and karaoke.

The Sights in a Day

A great start to the day is the irresistible combo of strong coffee and a lazy breakfast at **Anna Blume** (p136), preferably at a sidewalk table. Spend the rest of the morning strolling down to Kollwitzplatz and its side streets, popping into indie boutiques for fashions, furnishings, baby clothing, handmade chocolates and whatever else local hearts desire. Walk north via leafy Husemannstrasse to the lovely red-brick **Kulturbrauerei** (p133) and plunge into daily life in East Germany at the **Museum in der Kulturbrauerei** (p132).

Order a *Currywurst* (curried sausage) at **Konnopke's Imbiss** (p135) and decide for yourself whether the queue is justified. Put in a bit more shopping along Kastanienallee and Oderberger Strasse, then head over to the **Mauerpark** (p128) and try to visualise what it looked like when the Berlin Wall ran through it.

Make your way back to Kastanienallee and stake out a table beneath the towering chestnuts of **Prater** (p135), Berlin's oldest beer garden. For dinner, either walk around the corner to **Oderquelle** (p135) or book (weeks) ahead for **La Soupe Populaire** (p134), followed by cocktails at **Le Croco Bleu** (p136).

For a local's day in Prenzlauer Berg, see p128.

Local Life

Sundays Around the Mauerpark (p128)

Best of Berlin

Eating

Umami (p133)

La Soupe Populaire (p134)

Habba Habba (p133)

Bars

Deck 5 (p136)

Le Croco Bleu (p136)

Becketts Kopf (p136)

Weinerei (p135)

Getting There

S S-Bahn The main hub is Schönhauser Allee station (S8, S9, S41 and S42).

Tram The most useful line is the M1, which links to the Scheunenviertel and Museum Island via Schönhauser Allee and Kastanienallee.

U U-Bahn The U2 comes up from Alexanderplatz. The most central jumping-off point is Eberswalder Strasse station.

Local Life
Sundays Around the Mauerpark

Long-time locals, neo-Berliners, the international tourist brigade... everyone flocks to the Mauerpark on Sundays. It's a wild and wacky urban tapestry where a flea market, outdoor karaoke and artists provide entertainment and people gather for barbecues, basketball and boules. A graffiti-covered section of the Berlin Wall quietly looms above it all.

❶ Bright Beginnings

Start your day on Oderberger Strasse, with breakfast at **Hüftengold** (☎030-4171 4500; Oderberger Strasse 27) or waffles at **Kauf Dich Glücklich** (Oderberger Strasse 44) and admire the beautiful facades of the restored 19th-century townhouses that were saved from demolition in the late 1970s.

2 Coffee Deluxe

Yumi and Kiduk, the pioneers of the Third Wave Coffee craze in Berlin, make a mean cuppa java from beans freshly roasted in their tiny industrial-style cafe, **Bonanza Coffee Heroes** (www.bonanzacoffee.de; Oderberger Strasse 35; ⌚8.30am-7pm Mon-Fri, 10am-7pm Sat & Sun), and fed into a Synesso Cyncra, the 'Lamborghini' of espresso machines. Lines can be long, so bring patience.

3 Confronting Cold War History

During the Cold War, East clashed against West at Bernauer Strasse, now paralleled by the 1.4km-long **Gedenkstätte Berliner Mauer** (p74), a multimedia memorial that vividly illustrates the realities of life with the Berlin Wall. It starts at Schwedter Strasse. Even walking just a short stretch is an eye-opening experience.

4 Urban Archaeology

After a dose of history, you're now ready to join thrifty trinket hunters, bleary-eyed clubbers and excited visitors sifting for treasure at the vibrant **Mauerpark Flea Market** (www.mauerparkmarkt.de; Bernauer Strasse 63-64; ⌚10am-5pm Sun; S Eberwalder Strasse). Source new favourites among the retro threads, local-designer T-shirts, communist memorabilia, vintage vinyl and offbeat stuff. Ethnic food stands and beer gardens provide sustenance.

5 Bearpit Karaoke

On most summer Sundays, Berlin's best free entertainment kicks off around 3pm when Joe Hatchiban sets up his custom-made mobile karaoke unit in the Mauerpark's amphitheatre. As many as 2000 people cram onto the stone bleachers to cheer and clap for eager crooners ranging from giggling 11-year-olds to Broadway-calibre belters. Check Facebook for dates.

6 Falkplatz

Flashback to 1825 and picture Prussian soldiers parading around what is now a leafy park studded with ancient chestnut, oak, birch, ash and poplar trees. Relax on the grass and watch kids frolicking around the sea-lion fountain, then search for other animal sculptures tucked among the shrubs.

7 Burgermania

New York meets Berlin at the **Bird** (☎030-5105 3283; www.thebirdinberlin.com; Am Falkplatz 5; burgers €9.50-14, steaks from €16; ⌚6pm-midnight Mon-Fri, noon-midnight Sat & Sun), a buzzy gastropub known for its killer burgers. Sink your teeth into a dripping half-pounder made from freshly ground dry-aged Angus beef trapped between a toasted English muffin (yes, it's messy – that's what the kitchen roll is for!).

8 Northern Mauerpark

To escape the Mauerpark frenzy and see where locals relax, head north of the Gleimstrasse tunnel. You'll find an enchanting birch grove, an educational farm playground complete with barnyard animals, and the 'Schwedter Northface', a climbing wall operated by the German Alpine Club.

For reviews see

Sights	p132
Eating	p133
Drinking	p135
Shopping	p137

0 400 m
0 0.2 miles

A B C D E
1 2 3 4

Schivelbeiner Str
Dänenstr
Kopenhagener Str
Gleimstr
Gaudystr
Am Falkplatz
Falkplatz
Max-Schmeling-Halle
Friedrich Ludwig-Jahn Sportpark
Hinterlandmauer
Mauerpark
Schwedter Str
Cantianstr
Eberswalder Str
Eberswalder Str
Schönhauser Allee
Schönhauser Allee
Schönhauser Allee Arcaden
Schönhauser Allee
Wichertstr
Greifenhagener Str
Rodenbergstr
Stahlheimer Str
Stargarder Str
Pappelallee
Lychener Str
Raumerstr
Lettestr
Helmholtzplatz
Dunckerstr
Schliemannstr
Lychener Str
6
11
13
20
21
24

BERG
Museum in der Kulturbrauerei
Schwedter Str
Oderberger Str
7
4
Kulturbrauerei
Sredzkistr
Husemannstr
19
Christburger Str
Arkonaplatz
23
25
Schönhauser Allee
Rykestr
Ruppinerstr
Kastanienallee
Wörther Str
Kollwitzplatz
1
Marienburger Str
Fehrbelliner Str
Zionskirchplatz
12
3
Jüdischer Friedhof Schönhauser Allee
9
Knaackstr
5
10
17
Weinbergsweg
Choriner Str
Kollwitzstr
Prenzlauer Allee
Veteranenstr
Volkspark am Weinbergsweg
Schwedter Str
Metzer Str
Strassburger Str
Belforter Str
Teutoburger Platz
Senefelderplatz
Brunnenstr
22
Schönhauser Allee
Rosenthaler Platz
Saarbrücker Str
18
8
A
B
C
D
E
5
6
7
8

Sights

Kollwitzplatz

SQUARE

1 Map p130, D6

Triangular Kollwitzplatz is the epicentre of Prenzlauer Berg poshification. To pick up on the local vibe, linger with macchiato mamas and media daddies in a street cafe or join them at the organic **farmers market** (Kollwitzstrasse; noon-7pm Thu, 9am-4pm Sat). The park in the square's centre is tot heaven with three playgrounds plus a bronze sculpture of the artist Käthe Kollwitz for clambering on. (; S Senefelderplatz)

Museum in der Kulturbrauerei

MUSEUM

2 Map p130, D5

This new exhibit at the Kulturbrauerei uses original documents and objects (including a camper-style Trabi car) to teach the rest of us about daily life in East Germany. Four themed sections juxtapose the lofty aspirations of the socialist state with the sobering realities of material shortages, surveillance and oppression. Case studies show the different paths individuals took to deal – and cope – with their situation. (030-467 777 911; Knaackstrasse 97; admission free; 10am-6pm Tue, Wed & Fri-Sun, to 8pm Thu; S Eberswalder Strasse, M1, 12)

Farmers market, Kollwitzplatz

Jüdischer Friedhof Schönhauser Allee CEMETERY

3 Map p130, C7

Berlin's second Jewish cemetery opened in 1827 and hosts many well-known dearly departed, such as the artist Max Liebermann and the composer Giacomo Meyerbeer. It's a pretty place with dappled light filtering through big old trees and a sense of melancholy emanating from overgrown graves and toppled tombstones. (030-441 9824; Schönhauser Allee 23-25; 8am-4pm Mon-Thu, 7.30am-2.30pm Fri; S Senefelderplatz)

Kulturbrauerei HISTORIC BUILDING

4 Map p130, C5

The fanciful red-and-yellow brick buildings of this 19th-century brewery have been recycled into a cultural powerhouse with a small village's worth of venues, from concert and theatre halls to restaurants, nightclubs, stores and a multiscreen cinema. (030-4431 5152; www.kulturbrauerei.de; Schönhauser Allee 36; S Eberswalder Strasse, M1)

Eating

Umami VIETNAMESE €€

5 Map p130, E7

This beautifully designed restaurant made an instant splash thanks to its mellow Asian lounge vibe and inspired menu of Indochine favourites. Solid menu choices include the Deep Gold Beef with fresh mango strips and the Mekong's Surf & Turf with king prawn and tenderloin. For a special kick, don't miss the Saigon mule. (030-2886 0626; www.umami-restaurant.de; Knaackstrasse 16; mains €7.50-14; noon-11.30pm; S Senefelderplatz, M2)

Frau Mittenmang INTERNATIONAL €€

6 Map p130, E1

This unhurried, neighbourhood-adored restaurant with sidewalk bench seating delivers a daily changing roster of globally inspired dishes that sometimes push the culinary envelope, usually with delicious results. Hunker down at a polished wooden table and join locals for a meal, the house brew or a glass of excellent wine. Reservations essential. (030-444 5654; www.fraumittenmang.de; Rodenbergstrasse 37; mains €9-17; 6-11pm; S Schönhauser Allee, M1, Schönhauser Allee)

Habba Habba MIDDLE EASTERN €

7 Map p130, C5

The best wraps in town for our money, especially the one stuffed with pomegranate-marinated chicken and nutty buckwheat dressed in a minty yoghurt sauce. One bite and you're hooked. Vegan loyalists swear by the sesame-coated halloumi. Take away or score a seat on the raised porch. (030-3674 5726; www.habba-habba.de; Kastanienallee 15; dishes €4-8; 10am-10pm; ; M1, 12, Eberswalder Strasse)

La Soupe Populaire GERMAN €€

8 Map p130, D8

Local top toque Tim Raue's newest gastro destination embraces the soulful goodness of German home-cooking, with a best seller being his riff on *Königsberger Klopse* (veal meatballs in caper sauce). It's all served in an industrial-chic space within a defunct 19th-century brewery where patrons sit at vintage tables overlooking a gallery space showcasing changing contemporary art. (030-4431 9680; www.lasoupepopulaire.de; Prenzlauer Allee 242; mains €14-21; noon-midnight Thu-Sat; S Rosa-Luxemburg-Strasse, M2)

Lucky Leek VEGAN €€

9 Map p130, D7

Josita Hartanto not only knows how to coax maximum flavour out of the vegetable kingdom, but has a knack for combining them boldly and creatively. Even die-hard carnivores will likely swoon over such results as creamy wasabi-pea risotto, Seitan dumplings and asparagus ravioli. (030-6640 8710; www.lucky-leek.de; Kollwitzstrasse 54; mains €12-18; 6-11pm Wed-Sun; ; S Senefelderplatz)

Der Hahn ist tot! FRENCH €€

10 Map p130, B7

A French children's ditty inspired the curious name, which translates as 'The rooster is dead!' Here the deceased fowl is turned into coq au vin, the classic French country stew that's always on the menu at this pretension-free restaurant. Every night, staff dish up three four-course dinners, including a meat-free selection, at an unbeatable price. (030 6570 6756; www.der-hahn-ist-tot.de; Zionskirchstrasse 40; 4-course dinner €20; 7-11pm Tue-Sun; S Eberswalder Strasse, M1)

Zia Maria ITALIAN €

11 Map p130, E2

This shoebox-sized pizza kitchen gets mobbed at all hours for its freshly made crispy-crust pies. Go classic or choose from such eclectic toppings as wafer-thin prosciutto, nutmeg-laced artichokes or pungent Italian sausage. Two slices are enough to fill up most. (www.zia-maria.de; Pappelallee 32a; pizza slices €1.50-3.50; noon-11.30pm; S Schönhauser Allee, 12, Schönhauser Allee)

W - der Imbiss FUSION €

12 Map p130, B7

The love child of Italian and Indian cooking, W's signature naan pizza is freshly baked in the tandoor oven and decorated with such tasty meatless toppings as goats cheese, artichoke paste and guacamole. Enjoy it amid cheerful tiki decor alongside a healthy spirulina-laced apple juice. Or a beer from the fridge. (030-4435 2206; www.w-derimbiss.de; Kastanienallee 49; dishes €4-12; noon-midnight; ; S Rosenthaler Platz, M1)

Zum Schusterjungen GERMAN €€

13 Map p130, D4

At this rustic corner pub, authentic Berlin charm is doled out with as much abandon as the delish home ooking. Big platters of goulash, roast ork and *Sauerbraten* feed both ummy and soul, as do the regionally rewed Berliner Schusterjunge pilsner nd Märkischer Landmann black beer. (☎030-442 7654; www.zumschusterjungen. om; Danziger Strasse 9; mains €5-13; 11am-midnight; S Eberswalder Strasse)

)derquelle

GERMAN €€

14 Map p130, B5

t's always fun to pop by this woodsy esto and see what's inspired the chef to- lay. Most likely, it will be a well-crafted German meal, perhaps with a slight Mediterranean nuance. On the standard nenu, the crispy *Flammekuche* (Alsatian pizza) is a reliable standby. Best seat: on he sidewalk so you can keep an eye on he parade of passers-by. (☎030-4400 3080; www.oderquelle.de; Oderberger Strasse 27; mains €8-20, 3-course dinner €23.50; 6-11pm Mon-Sat, noon-11pm Sun; S Eberswal- der Strasse, M1, 12)

Konnopke's Imbiss

GERMAN €

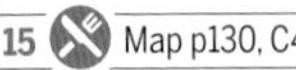

15 Map p130, C4

Brave the inevitable queue at this famous sausage kitchen, ensconced in the same spot below the elevated U-Bahn track since 1930, but now equipped with a heated pavilion and an English menu. The 'secret' sauce topping their classic *Currywurst* comes in a four-part heat scale from mild to wild. (☎030-442 7765; www.konnopke-imbiss.de; Schönhauser Allee 44a; sausages €1.40-1.90; 9am-8pm Mon-Fri, 11.30am-8pm Sat; S Eberswalder Strasse, M1, M10)

Local Life

Knaackstrasse Cafe Scene

Mere steps from Kollwitzplatz, pretty **Knaackstrasse** (Map p130, E7) is a quiet residential street with a row of charming cafes and restaurants perfect for people-watching while enjoying breakfast or a beer at a sunny sidewalk table. The round tower opposite is Berlin's oldest water tower (1877), now honeycombed with pie-sliced flats. In Nazi Germany, its machine room went through a sinister stint as an improvised prison and torture centre.

Drinking

Prater

BEER GARDEN

16 Map p130, C5

This place has seen beer-soaked nights since 1837, making it Berlin's oldest beer garden. It's kept much of its traditional charm and is still perfect for guzzling a custom-brewed Prater pilsner beneath the ancient chestnut trees (self-service). Kids can romp around the small play area. In foul weather or winter, the adjacent beer hall is a fine place to sample classic Berlin dishes (€8 to €19). (☎030-448 5688; www.pratergarten.de; Kastanienallee 7-9; noon-late Apr-Sep; S Eberswalder Strasse)

Weinerei

WINE BAR

17  Map p130, A7

This living-room-style wine bar works on the honour principle: you 'rent' a wine glass for €2, then help yourself to as much vino as you like and in the end decide what you want to pay. Please be fair and do not take advantage of this fantastic concept. (030-440 6983; www.weinerei.com; Veterananstrasse 14; 8pm-late; ; S Rosenthaler Platz, M1)

Le Croco Bleu

COCKTAIL BAR

18 Map p130, D8

Berlin cocktail luminary Gregor Scholl's newest 'laboratory' occupies the machine room of a defunct 19th-century brewery. Amid stuffed animals, mushroom tables and other whimsical Hansel-and-Gretel decor, you get to enjoy extravagant twists on time-tested classics. Fairy Floss – a Sazerac topped with absinthe-laced cotton candy – never fails to elicits oohs and aahs. (0177 443 2359; www.lecrocobleu.com; Prenzlauer Allee 242; 6pm-late Thu-Sat; S Rosa-Luxemburg-Strasse, M2)

Top Tip

Shopping Areas

Prenzlauer Berg is mercifully devoid of chains. Streets where indie boutiques thrive include **Kastanienallee** and **Oderberger Strasse** (Map p130, C5), **Stargarder Strasse** (Map p130, E3) and the streets around **Helmholtzplatz** (Map p130, E4). Most stores don't open until noon or later and close around 6pm or 7pm.

Anna Blume

CAFE

19 Map p130, E5

Potent java, homemade cakes and flowers from the attached shop perfume the art nouveau interior of this corner cafe named for a 1919 Dadaist poem by German artist Kurt Schwitters. In fine weather the sidewalk terrace is the best people-watching perch. Great for breakfast, especially the tiered tray for two. (030-4404 8749; www.cafe-anna-blume.de; Kollwitzstrasse 83; 8am-2am; S Eberswalder Strasse)

Becketts Kopf

COCKTAIL BAR

20 Map p130, D3

Past Samuel Beckett's portrait, the art of cocktail-making is taken very seriously. Settle into a heavy armchair in the warmly lit lounge and take your sweet time to peruse the extensive drinks menu. All the classics are accounted for, of course, as are such tempting specials as the mysterious gin- and bourbon-based Black Hawk. (0162 237 9418; www.becketts-kopf.de; Pappelallee 64; 8pm-2am Tue-Sun; S Schönhauser Allee, 12, Schönhauser Allee)

Deck 5

BAR

21 Map p130, D1

Soak up the rays at this beach bar in the sky while sinking your toes into tonnes of sand lugged to the top parking deck of the Schönhauser Arkaden mall. Take the lift from within the mall or walk up a never-ending flight of stairs from Greifenhagener Strasse. www.freiluftrebellen.de; Schönhauser Allee 30; 10am-midnight Mon-Sat, noon-midnight Sun, in good summer weather only; S Schönhauser Allee, M1, Schönhauser Allee)

Bassy
CLUB

22 Map p130, C8

Most punters here have a post-Woodstock birth date, but happily ride the retro wave at this trashy-charming concert and party den dedicated 'strictly' to pre-1969 sounds – surf music, rockabilly, swing and country among them. Concerts, burlesque cabaret and the infamous **Chantals House of Shame** (www.siteofshame.com; from 11pm Thu) gay party on Thursdays beef up the schedule. Dress...creatively. (030-3744 8020; www.bassy-club.de; Schönhauser Allee 176a; 9pm-late Wed, Fri & Sat; S Senefelderplatz)

Shopping

Flohmarkt am Arkonaplatz
MARKET

23 Map p130, A6

Surrounded by cafes perfect for carbo-loading, this smallish flea market lets you ride the retro frenzy with plenty of groovy furniture, accessories, clothing, vinyl and books, including some GDR-era stuff. It's easily combined with a visit to the nearby Flohmarkt am Mauerpark (p129). (www.mauerpark-markt.de; Arkonaplatz; 10am-4pm Sun; S Bernauer Strasse)

Ta(u)sche
ACCESSORIES

24 Map p130, D4

Heike Braun and Antje Strubels now sell their ingenious messenger-style bags around the world, but this is the store where it all began. Bags come in 11 sizes with exchangeable flaps that zip off and on in seconds. (030-4030 1770; www.tausche.de; Raumerstrasse 8; 10am-8pm Mon-Fri, to 6pm Sat; S Eberswalder Strasse)

Luxus International
GIFTS, SOUVENIRS

25 Map p130, C6

There's no shortage of creative spirits in Berlin, but not many of them can afford their own store. In comes Luxus International, a unique concept store that rents them a shelf or two to display their original designs: T-shirts, tote bags, ashtrays, lamps, candles, mugs etc. You never know what you'll find, but you can bet it's a Berlin original. (030-8643 5500; www.luxus-international.de; Kastanienallee 84; 11am-8pm Mon-Sat; S Eberswalder Strasse, M1)

VEB Orange
GIFTS, SOUVENIRS

26 Map p130, B5

Viva vintage! With its selection of the most beautiful things from the '60s and '70s, this place is a tangible reminder of how colourful, campy and fun home decor used to be. True to its name, many of the furnishings, accessories, lamps and fashions are orange in colour. (030-9788 6886; www.vebo-range.de; Oderberger Strasse 29; 10am-8pm Mon-Sat; S Eberswalder Strasse)

Top Sights
Schloss & Park Sanssouci

Getting There

24km southwest of the city (ABC ticket €3.20).

Trains It's 25 minutes rom Berlin-Hauptbahnhof or Zoologischer Garten to Potsdam-Hauptbahnhof

S-Bahn The S7 takes 40 minutes.

This glorious park-and-palace ensemble is what happens when a king has good taste, plenty of cash and access to the finest architects and artists of the day. Sanssouci was dreamed up by Frederick the Great (1712–86) and is anchored by the eponymous palace, built as a summer retreat in Potsdam, a quick train ride from Berlin. His great-great-nephew Friedrich Wilhelm IV (1795–1861) added a few more buildings. Unesco gave the entire thing World Heritage status in 1990.

Chinese House, Park Sanssouci

Don't Miss

Schloss Sanssouci

This rococo jewel of a **palace** (adult/concession incl audioguide €12/8; ⌚10am-6pm Tue-Sun Apr-Oct, 10am-5pm Nov-Mar; 🚌650, 695) sits above vine-draped terraces with Frederick the Great's grave nearby. Standouts on the audioguide tours include the petite library, the whimsically decorated concert hall and the domed Marble Hall.

Chinesisches Haus

The adorable clover-leaf-shaped **Chinese House** (admission €2; ⌚10am-6pm Tue-Sun May-Oct) is a shutterbug favourite thanks to an enchanting exterior of exotically dressed gilded figures sipping tea, dancing and playing musical instruments. Inside is a precious porcelain collection.

Bildergalerie

The **Picture Gallery** (adult/concession €6/5; ⌚10am-6pm Tue-Sun May-Oct) is Germany's oldest royal museum, resplendent in yellow and white marble and elaborate stuccowork. It shelters Frederick's collection of Old Masters, including Caravaggio's *Doubting Thomas*, Anton van Dyck's *Pentecost* and several works by Peter Paul Rubens.

Neues Palais

The **New Palace** (adult/concession with audio-guide €8/6; ⌚10am-6pm Wed-Mon Apr-Oct, to 5pm Nov-Mar) has made-to-impress dimensions, a central dome and a lavish exterior capped with a parade of sandstone figures. It was the final palace built by Frederick the Great, primarily for representational purposes. Only the last German Kaiser, Wilhelm II, actually used it as a residence (until 1918).

☎0331-969 4200

www.spsg.de

Maulbeerallee

day pass to all palaces adult/concession €19/14

🚌606, 695 from Potsdam Hauptbahnhof

☑ Top Tips

▶ For information, pop by the **Sanssouci Visitor Center** (An der Orangerie 1; ⌚8.30am-5.30pm Tue-Sun Apr-Oct, to 4.30pm Nov-Mar).

▶ Admission to Sanssouci Palace is limited and by timed ticket only. Book online to avoid wait times and/or disappointment.

▶ Most buildings are closed on Mondays.

Take a Break

In Park Sanssouci, the **Drachenhaus** (☎0331-505 3808; www.drachenhaus.de; Maulbeerallee 4; mains €7.50-23; ⌚11am-7pm or later Apr-Oct, to 6pm Tue-Sun Nov-Feb), a pagoda-style mini-palace, is a pleasant cafe-restaurant serving cakes and upmarket regional cuisine.

Orangerieschloss

The 300m-long Mediterranean-styled **Orangery Palace** (adult/concession €4/3; ⏲10am-6pm Tue-Sun May-Oct, Sat & Sun Apr) reflects Friedrich Wilhelm IV's love for all things Italian. Tours take in the **Raphaelsaal**, which brims with 19th-century copies of the famous painter's masterpieces, while the **tower** (admission €2) delivers sweeping park views.

Belvedere auf dem Klausberg

From the Orangery Palace, a tree-lined path forms a visual axis to this temple-like **pavilion** (admission €2; ⏲10am-6pm Sat & Sun May-Oct), which delivers a sweeping panorama of the park, lakes and Potsdam itself.

Neue Kammern

The **New Chambers** (adult/concession incl tour or audioguide €4/3; ⏲10am-6pm Tue-Sun Apr-Oct) was originally an orangery and later converted into a guesthouse. The interior drips with rococo opulence, most notably in the Ovidsaal, a grand ballroom with gilded reliefs depicting scenes from *Metamorphosis,* and in the Jasper Hall, drenched in precious stones and topped by a ceiling fresco starring Venus.

Park Charlottenhof

Laid out by Peter Lenńe for Friedrich Wilhelm IV, this park segues from Park Sanssouci but gets much fewer visitors. Buildings in this quiet corner bear the stamp of Karl Friedrich

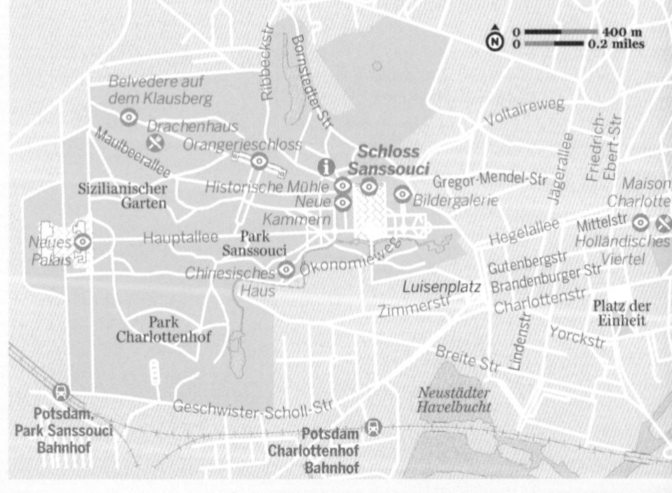

Schinkel, most notably the neoclassical **Schloss Charlottenhof** (Geschwister-Scholl-Strasse 34a; tour adult/concession €4/3; ⏲10am-6pm Tue-Sun May-Oct), modelled after a Roman villa, and the nearby **Roman Baths** (adult/concession €5/4; ⏲10am-6pm Tue-Sun mid-Apr–Oct), a picturesque ensemble of Italian country villas.

Historische Mühle

This is a functioning replica of the palace's original Dutch-style 18th-century **windmill** (Historical Mill; ☎0331-550 6851; www.spsg.de; Maulbeerallee 5; adult/concession €3/2; ⏲10am-6pm daily Apr-Oct, 10am-4pm Sat & Sun Nov & Jan-Mar). There's a shop on the ground floor, three exhibit floors detailing mill technology and a top-floor viewing platform.

Belvedere auf dem Klausberg

Nearby: Holländisches Viertel

To get a sense of Potsdam beyond the palaces, head east for about 1km via the pedestrianised Brandenburger Strasse shopping lane to the **Dutch Quarter**, a picturesque cluster of 134 gabled red-brick houses built around 1730 for Dutch workers invited to Potsdam by Friedrich Wilhelm I. The pint-size quarter has been done up beautifully and brims with galleries, cafes and restaurants. Mittelstrasse is especially scenic.

The Best of Berlin

Berlin's Best Walks

Berlin's Best...

Berliner Dom (p49)

Best Walks
Historical Highlights

The Walk

This walk checks off Berlin's blockbuster landmarks as it cuts right through the historic city centre, Mitte (literally 'Middle'). This is the birthplace and glamorous heart of Berlin, a high-octane cocktail of culture, architecture and commerce. You'll follow in the footsteps of kings and soldiers, marvel at grand architecture and stroll cobbled lanes, travel from the Middle Ages to the future and be awed by some of the world's finest works of art. Bring that camera!

Start Reichstag; U Bundestag, 100, TXL

Finish Nikolaiviertel; S Alexanderplatz, U Alexanderplatz, 100, 200, TXL

Length 3.5km; three hours

Take a Break

Cafe Einstein (www.einsteinudl.de; Unter den Linden 42; mains €9-18; 7am-10pm) makes for an arty pit stop. Wrap up the tour at **Brauhaus Georgbräu** (p51) in the Nikolaiviertel.

Reichstag Dome (p25)

1 Reichstag

The 1894 **Reichstag** (p24) is the historic anchor of Berlin's federal government quarter. The sparkling glass dome, added during the building's 1990s revamp, has become a shining beacon of unified Berlin.

2 Brandenburg Gate

The only remaining gate of Berlin's 18th-century town wall, the **Brandenburg Gate** (p26) became an involuntary neighbour of the Berlin Wall during the Cold War. It's now a cheery symbol of German reunification.

3 Unter den Linden

Originally a riding path linking the city palace with the royal hunting grounds in Tiergarten, **Unter den Linden** has been Berlin's showpiece road since the 18th century but is partly torn up thanks to the construction of a new U-Bahn line.

4 Gendarmenmarkt

Berlin's most beautiful square, **Gendarmenmarkt** (p32) is bookended by domed cathedrals with the famous Konzerthaus (Concert Hall) in between. The surrounding streets are lined with elegant hotels, restaurants and cocktail bars.

5 Museum Island

The sculpture-studded Palace Bridge leads to the twee Spree island whose northern half, **Museumsinsel**, is a Unesco-recognised treasure chest of art, sculpture and objects spread across five grand museums.

6 Humboldtforum

Opposite Museum Island, the massive Humboldtforum is taking shape. Its facade will mimic the old Prussian city palace, its modern interior will house museums and a library. Details at the **Humboldt-Box** (☎0180-503 0707; www.humboldt-box.com; admission €2; ⏱10am-7pm; 🚌100, 200, S Hausvogteiplatz).

7 Berliner Dom

Pompous and majestic inside and out, the **Berlin Cathedral** (p49) is a symbol of Prussian imperial power and blessed with artistic treasures, royal sarcophagi and nice views from the gallery.

8 Nikolaiviertel

With its cobbled lanes and higgledy-piggledy houses, the **Nikolai Quarter** may look medieval but was actually built to celebrate Berlin's 750th birthday in 1987.

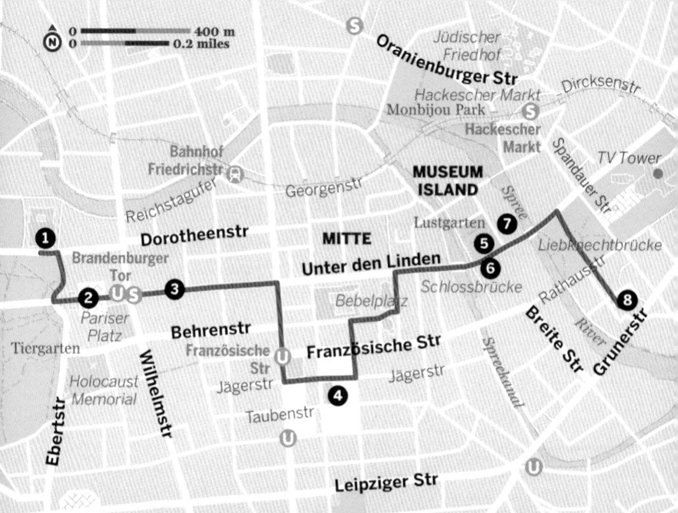

Best Walks
Walking the Wall

The Walk

Construction of the Berlin Wall began shortly after midnight on 13 August 1961. For the next 28 years this grim barrier divided a city and its people, becoming the most visible symbol of the Cold War. By now the city's halves have visually merged so perfectly that it takes a keen eye to tell East from West. To give you a sense of the period of division, this walk follows the most central section of the Berlin Wall. For a more in-depth experience, rent the multimedia **Mauerguide** (www.mauerguide.com) at Checkpoint Charlie.

Start Checkpoint Charlie; U Kochstrasse

Finish Parlament der Bäume; U Bundestag

Length 3km; two hours

Take a Break

Potsdamer Platz has the biggest concentration of eating and drinking options.

INGO JEZIERSKI/GETTY IMAGES ©

Remnants of the Berlin Wall

1 Checkpoint Charlie

As the third Allied checkpoint, **Checkpoint Charlie** (p65) got its name from the third letter in the NATO phonetic alphabet. Weeks after the Wall was built, US and Soviet tanks faced off here in one of the tensest moments of the Cold War.

2 Niederkirchner Strasse

Along Niederkirchner Strasse looms a 200m-long section of the original outer **border wall**. Scarred by souvenir hunters, it's now protected by a fence. The border strip was very narrow here, with the inner wall abutting such buildings as the former Nazi Air Force Ministry.

3 Watchtower

This is one of the few remaining GDR border **watchtowers**. Guards had to climb up a slim round shaft to reach the octagonal observation perch. Introduced in 1969, this cramped model was later replaced by larger square towers.

❹ Potsdamer Platz

Potsdamer Platz used to be a massive no-man's-land bisected by the Wall and a 'death strip' several hundred metres wide. Outside the northern S-Bahn station entrance are a few **Berlin Wall segments**.

❺ Brandenburg Gate

The **Brandenburg Gate** (p26) was where construction of the Wall began. Many heads of state gave speeches in front of it, perhaps most famously former US president Ronald Reagan who, in 1987, uttered the words: 'Mr Gorbachev – tear down this wall!'

❻ Art Installation

On the riverwalk level of the Marie-Elisabeth-Lüders-Haus, which houses the parliamentary library, an **art installation** by Ben Wagin features original Wall segments, each painted with a year and the number of people killed at the border in that year. If the door's not open, sneak a peek through the window.

❼ Parlament der Bäume

Wagin also masterminded the **Parliament of Trees**, an art installation/memorial consisting of trees, pieces of the former border fortification, memorial stones, pictures and text. The names of 258 victims are inscribed on slabs of granite.

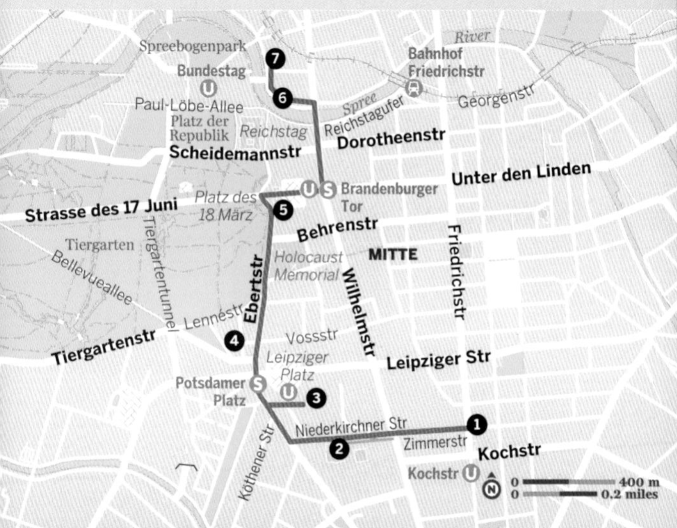

Best Walks A Leisurely Tiergarten Saunter

The Walk

Berlin's rulers used to hunt boar and pheasants in the forest-like Tiergarten until Peter Lenné landscaped the grounds in the 18th century. Today it's one of the world's largest urban parks, dotted with memorials and beer gardens, and is a popular place for strolling, jogging, picnicking and nude tanning.

Start Brandenburg Gate; S Brandenburger Tor U Brandenburger Tor

Finish Potsdamer Platz; S Potsdamer Platz, U Potsdamer Platz

Length 4km; 1½ to two hours

Take a Break

At **Cafe am Neuen See** (030-254 4930; www.cafeamneuensee.de; Lichtensteinallee 2; mains €9-20; 9am-11pm, beer garden from 11am Mon-Fri, from 10am Sat & Sun; 100, 200), a lakeside beer garden in the southwest of the park, cold beers go well with bratwurst, pretzels and pizza.

JOHN FREEMAN/GETTY IMAGES ©

Siegessäule (Victory Column)

1 Strasse des 17 Juni

The broad boulevard bisecting Tiergarten was named **Street of 17 June** in honour of the victims of the bloodily quashed 1953 workers' uprising in East Berlin. Back in the 16th century, the road linked two royal palaces; it was doubled in width and turned into a swastika-lined triumphal road under Hitler.

2 Sowjetisches Ehrenmal

Near the Brandenburg Gate end of the park, the **Soviet War Memorial** is flanked by two Russian T-34 tanks said to have been the first to enter the city in 1945. It was built by German workers on order of the Soviets and completed just months after the end of the war. More than 2000 Red Army soldiers are buried behind the colonnade.

3 Schloss Bellevue

A succession of German presidents have made their home in snowy-white **Bellevue Palace**.

The neoclassical pile was originally a pad for the youngest brother of King Frederick the Great, then became a school under Kaiser Wilhelm II and a museum of ethnology under the Nazis. It's closed to the public.

❹ Siegessäule

Engulfed by roundabout traffic, the 1873 **Victory Column** was erected to celebrate Prussian military victories and is now a prominent symbol of Berlin's gay community. What would Bismarck think of that? The gilded woman on top represents the goddess of victory and is featured prominently in the Wim Wenders movie *Wings of Desire*. Climb to the top to appreciate the park's dimensions.

❺ Rousseauinsel

One of Tiergarten's most idyllic spots is the **Rousseauinsel**, a teensy island in a placid pond that's a memorial to 18th-century French philosopher Jean-Jacques Rousseau. It was designed to resemble his actual burial site on an island near Paris. Just look for the stone pillar.

❻ Luiseninsel

Another enchanting place, **Luiseninsel** is a tranquil gated garden brimming with statues and redolent with seasonal flower beds. It was created after Napoleon's occupying troops left town in 1808 in celebration of the return from exile of the royal couple Friedrich Wilhelm III and Queen Luise.

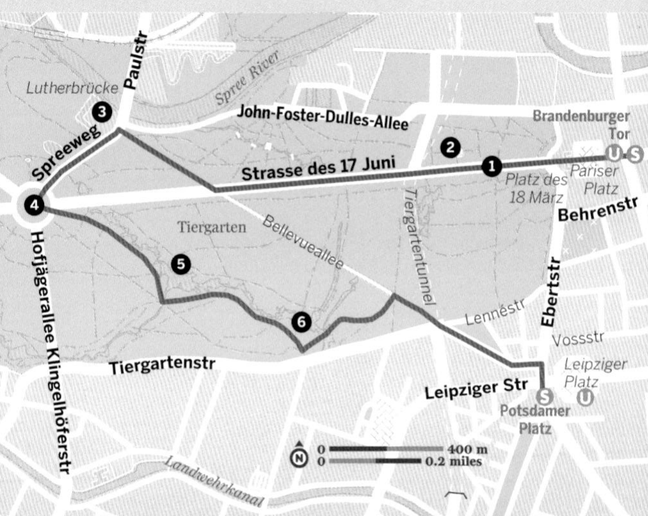

Best Museums

With more museums than rainy days (180 at last count), Berlin has an extraordinarily diverse cultural landscape that caters for just about every interest, be it art, film, history, nature, computers, antiquities or even *Currywurst* (a local snack). Many of them top the list of the city's must-see attractions – and not just for rainy days.

ARCHITECT: I. M. PEI; IMAGE: SIEGFRIED LAYDA/GETTY IMAGES

☑ Top Tips

- For many museums you can buy tickets in advance online, allowing you to skip the queues.
- Museum lovers should invest in the Museumspass Berlin (€24; available at participating museums) for one-time entry to about 50 museums on three consecutive days.

Museum Island

Museum Island, a Unesco World Heritage Site, presents over 6000 years of art and cultural history in five massive repositories built between 1830 and 1930. Marvel at antiquities from Greece, Egypt, Babylon, Rome and other ancient societies at the Altes Museum, the Pergamonmuseum and the Neues Museum, 19th-century paintings at the Alte Nationalgalerie and European sculpture at the Bodemuseum.

History Museums

From its humble medieval beginnings, Berlin's history – and especially its key role in major events of the 20th century – is a rich and endlessly fascinating tapestry. It's also extremely well documented, in numerous museums, memorial sites and monuments, many of them in original historic locations and most of them free.

Nationalgalerie Berlin

The National Gallery is a top-ranked collection of mostly European art from the 19th century to today, presented in six locations. The Alte Nationalgalerie specialises in neoclassical, romantic, impressionist and early modernist art; at the Hamburger Bahnhof the spotlight is on international contemporary art; the Museum Berggruen focuses on Picasso; and the Sammlung Scharf-Gerstenberg on surrealist art. Two additional museums, the New National Gallery and the Friedrichswerdersche Kirche, are currently closed for renovation.

Left: Deutsches Historisches Museum; Above: Altes Museum

Best History Museums

Deutsches Historisches Museum Comprehensive journey through 2000 years of Germany's turbulent past. (p32)

Jüdisches Museum Goes beyond the Holocaust in tracing the history of Jews in Germany. (p62)

DDR Museum Engaging look at daily life behind the Iron Curtain. (p49)

Best Niche Museums

Bröhan Museum Beautiful objects and furniture from the art deco, art nouveau and functionalist periods. (p98)

Museum für Naturkunde Meet giant dinos in Berlin's own 'Jurassic Park'. (p172)

Museum für Film und Fernsehen An entertaining romp through German celluloid history. (p61)

Museum für Fotografie Spotlight on fashion and lifestyle photographer Helmut Newton. (p90)

Best Antiquities

Pergamonmuseum Treasure trove of monumental architecture from ancient civilisations. (p42)

Altes Museum Gorgeous Schinkel building sheltering priceless antique art and sculpture. (p49)

Neues Museum Pay your respects to Egyptian queen Nefertiti and her entourage. (p46)

Worth a Trip

The former head office of the GDR's Ministry for State Security (Stasi) is now the **Stasimuseum Berlin** (030-553 6854; www.stasimuseum.de; Haus 1, Ruschestrasse 103; adult/concession €5/4; 10am-6pm Mon-Fri, noon-6pm Sat & Sun; S Magdalenenstrasse), where you can see a prisoner transport van, cunningly low-tech surveillance devices (hidden in watering cans, rocks, even neckties) and the obsessively neat offices of Stasi chief Erich Mielke.

Best Architecture

After visiting the German capital in 1891, Mark Twain remarked, 'Berlin is the newest city I've ever seen'. True then, still true now. Destruction and division have ensured that today's city is essentially a creation of modern times, a showcase of 20th-century styles with only surviving vestiges of earlier times.

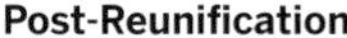

Post-Reunification

Reunification presented Berlin with both the challenge and the opportunity to redefine itself architecturally. With the Wall gone, huge gashes of empty space opened where the city's halves were to be rejoined. The grandest of the post-1990 developments is Potsdamer Platz, a contemporary interpretation of the famous historic square. Other recent architectural standouts include the Bundeskanzleramt (Federal Chancellery) and the Jüdisches Museum.

The Schinkel Touch

It was Karl Friedrich Schinkel (1781–1841) who stamped his imprimatur on the face of Prussian Berlin. The most prominent architect of German neoclassicism, he strove for the perfect balance between functionality and beauty, achieved through clear lines, symmetry and an impeccable sense of aesthetics.

The 1920s & the Bauhaus

The spirit of innovation brought some of the finest avant-garde architects to Berlin in the 1920s, including Le Corbusier, Ludwig Mies van der Rohe and Hans Scharoun. Their association later evolved into the Bauhaus, which used practical anti-elitist principles to unite form and function and had a profound effect on modern aesthetics.

Best of Schinkel

Altes Museum The grand colonnaded front inspired by a philosopher's school in Athens is considered Schinkel's most mature work. (p49)

Konzerthaus Berlin A sweeping staircase leads to a raised columned portico in this famous concert hall. (p38)

Neue Wache This royal guardhouse turned antiwar memorial was Schinkel's first Berlin commission. (p33)

Best Prussian

Brandenburg Gate This royal city gate is Germany's best-known landmark. (p26)

Left: Konzerthaus Berlin; Above: Berliner Dom

Schloss Charlottenburg Pretty Prussian power display. (p97)

Schloss Sanssouci Frederick the Great's rococo retreat. (p139)

Berliner Dom Former royal court church in exuberant Italian Renaissance style. (p49)

Best Post-WWII

Berliner Philharmonie This eccentric concert hall is Hans Scharoun's modernist masterpiece. (p69)

Haus der Kulturen der Welt Avant-garde structure with gravity-defying sculptural roof. (p35)

Best Post-1989

Jüdisches Museum Daniel Libeskind's zigzag-shaped architectural metaphor for Jewish history. (p62)

Neues Museum David Chipperfield's reconstructed New Museum ingeniously blends old and new. (p46)

Sony Center Helmut Jahn's svelte glass-and-steel complex is the most striking on Potsdamer Platz. (p61)

Worth a Trip

Built by the Nazis for the 1936 Olympic Games, the **Olympic Stadium** (☎030-2500 2322; www.olympiastadion-berlin.de; Olympischer Platz 3; adult/concession self-guided tour €7/5, guided general tour €10/8, Hertha BSC tour €11/9; check website; Olympiastadion) was completely modernised for the 2006 FIFA World Cup when its bombastic bulk was softened by the addition of a spidery oval roof. It hosts soccer games, concerts and mega-events and can be toured on non-event days.

Best Historical Sites

In Berlin the past is always present. Strolling around boulevards and neighbourhoods, you can't help but pass legendary sights that take you back to the era of Prussian glory, the dark ages of the Third Reich, the tense period of the Cold War and the euphoria of reunification.

The Age of Prussia

Berlin has been a royal residence ever since Elector Friedrich III was elevated to King Friedrich I in 1701. This promotion significantly shaped the city, which blossomed under Frederick the Great, who sought greatness as much on the battlefield as through building. In the 19th century, Prussia weathered revolutions and industrialisation to forge the creation of the German Reich, which lasted until the monarchy's demise in 1918.

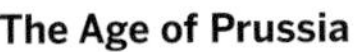

Berlin under the Nazi Nadir

No other political power shaped the 20th century as much as Nazi Germany. The megalomania of Hitler and his henchmen wrought destruction upon much of Europe, bringing death to at least 50 million people, and forever realigned the world order. Few original sites remain, but memorials and museums keep the horror in focus.

Cold War Chills

After WWII, Germany fell into the crosshairs of the Cold War, a country divided along ideological lines by the victorious powers, its internal border marked by fences and a wall. Just how differently the two countries developed is still palpable in Berlin, expressed not only through Berlin Wall remnants such as the East Side Gallery but also through vastly different urban planning and architectural styles.

DAVID CLAPP/GETTY IMAGES ©

Best of Prussian Pomp

Brandenburg Gate This much photographed triumphal arch is Germany's most iconic national symbol. (p26)

Reichstag Stand in awe of history at the palatial home of the German parliament. (p24)

Schloss Charlottenburg Prussian palace providing a glimpse into the lifestyles of the rich and royal. (p97)

Siegessäule A giant gilded goddess crowns the top of the soaring Victory Column. (p149)

Left: Holocaust Memorial; Above: Reichstag

Best of Red Berlin

East Side Gallery The longest remaining stretch of the Berlin Wall is an art canvas. (p118)

Gedenkstätte Berliner Mauer Germany's central memorial to the victims of the Wall. (p129)

Karl-Marx-Allee East Berlin's pompous yet impressive main boulevard and showpiece of socialist architecture. (p122)

Tränenpalast Learn about the personal toll Germany's division took on ordinary citizens. (p32)

Checkpoint Charlie The famous border crossing was a Cold War hotspot. (p65)

Best of WWII History

Holocaust Memorial Commemorates the unspeakable horrors of the WWII Jewish genocide. (p28)

Topographie des Terrors Peels away the many layers of brutality of the Nazi state. (p65)

Gedenkstätte Deutscher Widerstand Commemorates the brave men and women of the German Nazi resistance. (p66)

Worth a Trip

Victims of persecution by the GDR-era Ministry for State Security (Stasi) often ended up in the grim **Stasi Prison** (Gedenkstätte Hohenschönhausen; http://en.stiftung-hsh.de; Genslerstrasse 66; adult/concession €5/2.50; English tours 2.30pm Wed, Sat & Sun, German tours daily; M5 to Freienwalder Strasse). Tours reveal the full extent of the terror and cruelty perpetrated by this sinister institution upon thousands of suspected regime opponents, many of them utterly innocent.

Best Tours

If you're a Berlin first-timer, letting someone else show you around is a great way to get your bearings, see the key sights quickly and obtain a general understanding of the city. All manner of explorations – from generic city bus tours to special-interest outings – are available.

Walking & Cycling Tours

Several companies offer English-language general city explorations and themed tours (eg Third Reich, Cold War, Potsdam) that don't require reservations – you just show up at the designated meeting point. Since these may change, check online for the latest or look for flyers in hotel or hostel lobbies. Some guides work for tips only but the better tours cost between €10 and €15.

Boat Tours

A lovely way to experience Berlin on a warm day is from the deck of a boat cruising the city's rivers, canals and lakes. Tours range from one-hour spins around the historic centre (from €12) to longer trips to Schloss Charlottenburg and beyond (from €15). Most offer live commentary in English and German and sell refreshments on board. Embarkation points cluster around Museum Island or check the website of **Stern und Kreisschiffahrt** (☎030-536 3600; www.sternundkreis.de; Treptower Park).

Bus Tours

Colourful buses tick off the key sights on two-hour loops with basic taped commentary in multiple languages. You're free to get off and back on at any of the stops. They depart roughly every 15 or 30 minutes between 10am and 5pm or 6pm daily; tickets cost €10 to €20. Several companies have a terminus along Kurfürstendamm.

Top Tips

▶ Get a crash course in 'Berlin-ology' by hopping on the upper deck of public **bus 100 or 200** (€2.60) at Zoologischer Garten or Alexanderplatz and letting the landmarks whoosh by.

▶ For a DIY walk along the Berlin Wall, rent a multimedia **Mauerguide** (www.mauerguide.com) from Checkpoint Charlie, the Berlin Wall Memorial or inside the Brandenburger Tor U-Bahn station.

Best Walking & Cycling Tours

Alternative Berlin Tours (p110) Pay-what-you-can urban and subculture tours, plus a street

Boat tour, Spree River

art workshop, an ecotour and an anti-pub crawl.

Fat Tire Bike Tours (☎030-2404 7991; www.fattirebiketours.com/berlin; Panoramastrasse 1a; adult/concession €24/22) Classic city, Nazi and Cold War bicycle tours (e-bikes available) plus the offbeat, alternative 'Raw' tour.

Berlin Walks (☎030-301 9194; www.berlinwalks.de; adult €12-15, concession €10-12) Get under the city's historical skin with the expert guides of Berlin's oldest English-language walking tour company.

Brewer's Berlin Tours (☎0177 388 1537; www.brewersberlintours.com; adult/concession €15/12) Purveyors of the epic all-day Best of Berlin tour and shorter donation-based 'express' tours.

Best Speciality Tours

Berliner Unterwelten (☎030-4991 0517; www.berliner-unterwelten.de; adult/concession €10/8) Explore Berlin's dark underbelly by picking your way past heavy steel doors, hospital beds and WWII detritus on a tour of WWII-era bunkers, shelters and tunnels.

Berlin Music Tours (☎030-3087 5633; www.musictours-berlin.com; bus/walking tours in German €29/12; ⏲bus tour 12.30pm Sat, walking tour 2pm Sun) This multimedia bus tour gives you the low-down on the last 40 years of Berlin's music history along with the scoop on who's rocking the city now. Also: private minibus tours, and walking tours of the Hansa recording studios.

Trabi Safari (☎030-2759 2273; www.trabi-safari.de; Zimmerstrasse 97; per person €34-60, Wall Ride €79-89) Catch the *Good Bye, Lenin!* vibe on tours around Berlin in a convoy of East German–made Trabant cars (Trabi; you can drive or be a passenger) as live commentary is piped into your vehicle. Drivers need to bring their license. New: Mustang safaris around the former US sector in West Berlin.

Berlinagenten (☎030-4372 0701; www.berlinagenten.com) Get a handle on all facets of Berlin's urban lifestyle with an insider private guide who opens doors to hot and/or secret bars, boutiques, restaurants, clubs, private homes and sights. Tours include the 'Gastro Rallye' for the ultimate foodie.

Best Art

Art aficionados will find their compass on perpetual spin in Berlin. Home to 440 galleries, scores of world-class collections and some 10,000 international artists, it has assumed a pole position on the global artistic circuit.

Getting Visual

The **Galleries Association of Berlin** (www.berliner-galerien.de) counts some 440 galleries within the city, but there are at least 200 non-commercial showrooms and off-spaces that regularly show new exhibitions. Although the orientation is global, it's well worth keeping an eye out for the latest works by major contemporary artists living and working in Berlin, including Thomas Demand, Jonathan Meese, Isa Genzken, Tino Seghal and the duo Ingar Dragset and Michael Elmgreen.

Gallery Quarters

Internationally renowned galleries like Eigen + Art, neugerriemschneider and Kicken cluster in the Scheunenviertel, especially along Linienstrasse and Auguststrasse. Standouts in western Berlin's traditional gallery district around Savignyplatz include Galerie Max Hetzer and Galerie Buchholz. Near Checkpoint Charlie, notable galleries hold forth on Zimmerstrasse, Charlottenstrasse and Markgrafenstrasse, including Galerie Thomas Schulte and Galerie Barbara Thumm. Heavy hitters along gritty Potsdamer Strasse south of Potsdamer Platz are Galerie Klosterfelde and Galerie Arndt.

Best Art Events

Berlin Biennale (www.berlinbiennale.de)

Gallery Weekend (www.gallery-weekend-berlin.de)

☑ Top Tips

- The **Museumspass Berlin** (€24) buys entry to about 50 museums on three consecutive days. Available at participating museums and the tourist offices.
- Check out the online magazine **Berlin Art Link** (www.berlinartlink.com).
- **GoArt** (www.goart-berlin.de) demystifies Berlin's art scene on customised tours of private collections, artist studios, galleries and street art locations.

Best Art Museums

Gemäldegalerie Sweeping survey of Old Masters from Germany, Italy,

Left: Alte Nationalgalerie; Above: Neue Nationalgalerie (p66)

France, Spain and the Netherlands. (p56)

Hamburger Bahnhof Warhol, Beuys and Twombly are among the hotshots in this brilliantly converted train station. (p78)

Alte Nationalgalerie Showcase of first-rate 19th-century art by leading German romantics and realists. (p51)

Best Contemporary Galleries

Sammlung Boros Prebook early for this stunning cutting-edge private collection housed in a WWII bunker. (p78)

Kunsthalle Deutsche Bank Shines the spotlight on the emerging art scenes in non-Western countries. (p35)

KW Institute for Contemporary Art Well-respected shows reflecting the latest trends in art. (p81)

Best Niche Collections

Museum Berggruen Priceless Picassos, plus works by Klee and Giacometti. (p98)

Sammlung Scharf-Gerstenberg Enter the surreal fantasy worlds of Goya, Magritte, Max Ernst and other giants of the genre. (p98)

Käthe-Kollwitz-Museum Representative collection of works by Germany's greatest female artist, famous for her haunting depictions of war and human loss and suffering. (p91)

Worth a Trip

In the southwestern suburb of Grunewald, about 7km from the city centre, the forest-framed **Brücke-Museum** (☎030-831 2029; www.bruecke-museum.de; Bussardsteig 9; adult/concession €5/3; ⏰11am-5pm Wed-Mon; S Oskar-Helene-Heim, then bus 115 to Pücklerstrasse) focuses on works by Karl Schmidt-Rottluff, Ernst Ludwig Kirchner and other members of The Bridge, Germany's first modern-artist group, founded in 1905.

Best Eating

If you crave traditional comfort food, you'll certainly find plenty of places in Berlin to indulge in roast pork knuckles, smoked pork chops or calves liver. These days, though, 'typical' local fare is lighter, healthier, creative and more likely to come from gourmet kitchens, organic eateries and a UN worth of ethnic restaurants, including 13 that flaunt Michelin stars.

Modern German

The organic, slow-food and locavore movements have inspired a new generation of Berlin chefs to let seasonal-regional-organic ingredients steer their menus. This has added pizzazz to classic, time-tested recipes by making them lighter and more creative.

Fast-Food Faves

The humble *Currywurst* is a sliced, subtly spiced sausage swimming in tomato sauce and dusted with curry powder. The doner kebab is a legacy of Berlin's vast Turkish community.

New Trends

Food trucks and street food have finally come to Berlin. Plug into the scene at the weekly **Street Food Thursday** (p108) at Markthalle Neun in Kreuzberg or check for upcoming events hosted by **Bite Club** (www.biteclub.de), **Burgers & Hip Hop** (www.facebook.com/burgersandhiphop) and **Beer&Beef** (www.facebook.com/BeerBeefFestival). Vegan and vegetarian eateries have also been sprouting faster than alfalfa and serve inspired menus that leave the staple veggie or tofu burger in the dust. Locals have also developed an obsession with the hunt for the perfect burger, and hardly a day seems to pass without the opening of yet another gourmet pattie temple.

☑ Top Tips

▶ Reservations are recommended, especially for dinner and at weekends. Many restaurant websites offer online booking.

▶ Many cafes and restaurants offer value-priced two- or three-course 'business' lunches on weekdays.

Best Traditional German

Max und Moritz Hearty fare and local brew in quaint century-old pub. (p108)

Augustiner am Gendarmenmarkt Go the whole hog at this famous Munich beer-hall transplant. (p36)

La Soupe Populaire

Zur Letzten Instanz Has done a roaring trade with local rib-stickers since 1621. (p51)

Best Modern German

La Soupe Populaire German classics taken to new levels in an ex-brewery. (p134)

Restaurant am Steinplatz Eclectic ingredients find their destinations in delectable creations. (p92)

Katz Orange This 'cat' fancies anything regional, seasonal and creative amid chic country decor. (p81)

Pauly Saal Time-honoured regional dishes reinterpreted in modern Michelin-decorated fashion. (p81)

Best Ethnic Eateries

Defne Turkish delights beyond the doner kebab. (p108)

Muret La Barba Meals have all the flavours of Italy locked inside them. (p83)

Umami Vietnamese food so perky it may get you off your Prozac. (p133)

Good Friends Berlin's best Chinese restaurant. (p92)

Best Quick Eats

Burgermeister Patty-and-bun joint in a historic toilet. Really. (p109)

Habba Habba Unconventional, flavour-packed and meatless Middle Eastern wraps. (p133)

Curry 36 Cult *Currywurst* purveyor. (p109)

Best Vegan & Vegetarian

Cookies Cream Hidden herbivore haven. (p36)

Mio Matto Pizza and pasta with a gourmet vegan twist. (p122)

Lucky Leek Richly satisfying meat-free dishes in stylish minimalist haunt. (p134)

Best Shopping

Berlin is a great place to shop, and we're definitely not talking malls and chains. The city's appetite for the individual manifests itself in small neighbourhood boutiques and buzzing markets that are a pleasure to explore. Shopping here is as much about mental and visual stimulus as it is about actually spending your cash, no matter whether you're frugal or a power-shopper.

Where to Shop

Berlin's main shopping boulevard is Kurfürstendamm (Ku'damm), which is largely the domain of mainstream retailers (H&M to Prada). Its extension, Tauentzienstrasse, is anchored by KaDeWe, continental Europe's largest department store. Standouts among the city's dozens of shopping centres are the concept mall Bikini Berlin and the vast new Mall of Berlin at Leipziger Platz.

Getting the most out of shopping in Berlin, though, means venturing off the high street and into the *Kieze* (neighbourhoods). This is where you'll discover a cosmopolitan cocktail of indie boutiques stirred by the city's zest for life, envelope-pushing energy and entrepreneurial spirit.

Opening Hours

Department stores, supermarkets and shops in major commercial districts (such as Kurfürstendamm) and malls usually open at 10am and close at 8pm or later. Boutiques and other smaller shops keep flexible hours, opening sometime mid-morning and generally closing at 7pm, sometimes 4pm on Saturday. Stores are closed on Sunday, except for some bakeries, supermarkets, flower shops and souvenir shops.

☑ Top Tips

- Most stores, especially smaller ones, do not accept credit cards.
- Head to Berlin's fabulous flea markets on Sunday..

Best Bookstores

Dussmann – Das Kulturkaufhaus The mother lode of books and music, with late opening hours. (p39)

Another Country Quirky English-language book-store/library/community living room. (p113)

Best Markets

Flohmarkt am Mauerpark Crowded as hell but still urban archaeology at its finest and funnest. (p129)

KaDeWe department store

Türkenmarkt Bazaarlike canalside market with bargain-price produce and Mediterranean deli fare. (p115)

Boxhagener Platz Treasure-hunting grounds with plenty of entertainment, cafes and people-watching. (p125)

Best Made in Berlin

ausberlin Music, clothing, jewellery, books and knick-knacks for scene-savvy label hunters. (p53)

Butterflysoulfire Avant-garde fashion label that gets minimalist elegance right. (p85)

Bonbonmacherei Find a new favourite in this old-fashioned candy kitchen. (p84)

Ta(u)sche Ingenious messenger bags with changeable flaps to lug your Berlin purchases. (p137)

Ampelmann Galerie Berlin's iconic traffic-light man on T-shirts, towels and more. (p85)

Best Food & Drink

KaDeWe Food Hall Mind-boggling bonanza of gourmet treats from around the world. (p95)

Markthalle Neun Revitalised historic market hall serving global bites on Street Food Thursday. (p108)

Fassbender & Rausch The finest pralines and truffles, plus Berlin landmarks built of chocolate. (p39)

1. Absinth Depot Berlin Make a date with the 'green fairy' at this eccentric depot. (p85)

Best Malls & Department Stores

Bikini Berlin Germany's first concept mall in revitalised 1950s landmark. (p94)

LP12 Mall of Berlin New high-end shopping quarter with 270 stores. (p69)

Galeries Lafayette French *'je ne sais quoi'* in uberstylish building by Jean Nouvel. (p39)

KaDeWe The ultimate consumer temple has everything every heart desires. (p95)

Best Bars

With its well-deserved reputation as one of Europe's primo party capitals, Berlin offers a thousand and one scenarios for getting your cocktails and kicks (or wine or beer, for that matter). Kreuzberg and Friedrichshain have the edgier venues, while Mitte teems with swish drinking dens guarded by doorstaff. Bars out west are more suited for date nights than dedicated drink a thons.

Etiquette

Table service is common in German bars and pubs; you shouldn't order at the bar unless you intend to hang out there or there's a sign saying *Selbstbedienung* (self-service). Note that in bars with live DJs, €1 or €2 is usually added to the cost of your first drink. Drinking in public is legal and widely practised, especially around party zones. Try to be civilised about it, though: no puking on the U-Bahn, please!

Drinking Trends

Not surprisingly, beer – especially Pils and Weizenbier (wheat beer) – is big in Berlin and most places pour a variety of national and imported brews. In general, though, regionally produced beverages are gaining in popularity. Look for craft beers by Rollberger, Heidenpeters, Vagabund, Flessa Bräu and Bierfabrik Berlin; vodka by Our/Berlin; Korn (a premium schnapps) by Berliner Brandstifter; or cider by Original Berliner Cidre. A new crop of dedicated wine bars and cocktail caverns has also notably elevated the 'liquid art' scene of late.

☑ Top Tips

- The line between cafe and bar is often blurred, with many places changing stripes as the hands move around the clock.
- Alcohol is served (and consumed) pretty much all day, and many bars keep pouring until the last tippler leaves.
- Some bars and pubs run happy hours, usually from 6pm to 9pm.

Best Beer Gardens

Café am Neuen See
Beer and pretzels in Tiergarten park. (p148)

Terrace, Monkey Bar

Prater Berlin's oldest beer garden. (p135)

Golgatha Alfresco charmer on the Kreuzberg, Berlin's highest natural hill. (p71)

Best Cocktail Bars

Schwarze Traube Pint-size drinking parlour serving bespoke cocktails. (p110)

Becketts Kopf Wait for Godot while sipping supreme classics and seasonal inspirations. (p136)

Le Croco Bleu Artful potions in an industrial fairy-tale forest at an ex-brewery. (p136)

Butcher's Clandestine drinking den hidden in a sausage shop. (p83)

Best Summertime Bars

Strandbar Mitte Berlin's original beach bar with views of Museum Island. (p52)

Freischwimmer Canal-side setting favoured by chillers and party people. (p110)

Club der Visionäre Boatshed turned party pen with DJs who know the groove. (p110)

Klunkerkranich Hipster spot with garden atop Neukölln shopping centre. (p115)

Best Bars with a View

House of Weekend Cocktails and barbecue (almost) at eye level with the TV Tower. (p52)

Solar Stylish and romantic with mellow sounds. (p69)

Monkey Bar Exotic tiki drinks with a view of the baboons of the Berlin Zoo. (p94)

Deck 5 Count the steeples from this bar atop a shopping mall. (p136)

Best Wine Bars

Vin Aqua Vin Eliminates wine bar trepidation with casual vibe and wallet-friendly vintages. (p115)

Weinerei Works on the honour system: you drink, then decide how much to pay. (p135)

Otto Rink For relaxed oenophiles with a penchant for German wines. (p105)

Best Clubs

Berlin is Germany's club capital, the city where techno came of age, the living heart of the European electronic scene and the spiritual home of the lost weekend. With a sound spectrum from minimal techno to fist-pumping hip-hop and tango, finding a party to match your mood shouldn't be a tall order.

When to Go

Berlin's notoriously late nights have gotten even later of late. Most clubs and parties don't kick into high gear until about 2am and some go nonstop from Friday night to Monday morning. Some folks put in a good night's sleep, then hit the dance floor when other people head for Sunday church.

At the Door

Top clubs charge €12 or €15 for admission, but elsewhere €3 to €10 is typical. Doors can be tough on busy nights at top clubs like Berghain/Panorama Bar, Watergate and the Pearl but, overall, making it past the bouncer is still relatively relaxed. Individual style generally beats high heels and Armani, and if your attitude is right, age rarely matters. As elsewhere, large groups (even mixed ones) have a lower chance of getting in, so split up if you can.

Spinmeisters

With so many top electro DJs living in Berlin – and others happy to visit – the city is a virtual musical testing lab and line-ups are often amazing. DJ royalty to watch out for includes Ellen Allien, Tama Sumo, Sammy Dee, Ben Klock, Sascha Funke, Marcel Dettmann, Tale of Us, Paul Kalkbrenner, Moderat, Henrik Schwarz, M.A.N.D.Y, Tiefschwarz, Paul van Dyk, Booka Shade, Richie Hawtin and too many more to mention.

☑ Top Tips

- Good blogs and websites: www.residentadvisor.com, www.theclubmap.com, www.exberliner.de, www.mitvergnuegen.com, www.zitty.de, www.tip-berlin.de
- Don't bother showing up before 1am unless you want to have a conversation with a bored bartender.
- If you have to queue, be respectful, don't drink and don't talk too loudly. Don't arrive wasted or in big groups.

Left: Kaffee Burger; Above: Watergate

Best Electro

Berghain Hyped but still happening Holy Grail of techno clubs with DJ royalty every weekend. (p124)

Watergate Two floors, a stunning riverside setting and plenty of eye candy. (p111)

://about blank Wild, trashy, unpredictable – with an enchanting garden for daytime chilling. (p124)

Prince Charles Bar-club combo spinning fine electro in a former swimming pool. (p111)

Suicide Circus Top techno line-ups on indoor/outdoor floors in former warehouse. (p124)

Best Non-Electro

Clärchens Ballhaus Hipsters mix it up with grannies for tango and jitterbug in a kitsch-glam 1913 ballroom. (p83)

Kaffee Burger Home of readings, parties, concerts and endless nights of delicious debauchery. (p83)

Pearl Well-heeled weekend warriors press the flesh at this tricked-out party pen. (p95)

Worth a Trip

On summer weekends, **Sisyphos** (030-9836 6839; www.sisyphos-berlin.net; Hauptstrasse 15; hours vary, usually Fri & Sat Jun-Aug, weather permitting; 21, Ostkreuz), in an old dog-food factory about 2km southeast of S-Bahn station Ostkreuz, turns into a hedonistic party village that proves that Berlin can still 'do underground'. Climb to the viewing platform, which includes a pond and a fire truck. Electro dominates the turntables on the main floor with its great sound system. Relaxed door.

Best Gay & Lesbian

Berlin's legendary liberalism has spawned one of the world's biggest, most divine and diverse GLBT playgrounds. Anything goes in 'Homopolis' (and we do mean anything!), from the highbrow to the hands-on, the bourgeois to the bizarre, the mainstream to the flamboyant. Except for the most hardcore places, gay spots get their share of opposite-sex and straight patrons.

Top Tips

- The weekly freebie magazine **Siegessäule** (www.siegessaeule.de, in German) is Berlin's lesbigay 'bible'.
- Free English/German booklet and website **Out in Berlin** (www.out-in-berlin.de) is an indispensable guide.
- Good websites: www.discodamaged.net, www.patroc.de/berlin, www.gayberlin4u.com, http://berlin.gaycities.com

Gay Neighbourhoods

The area around Nollendorfplatz in Schöneberg (Motzstrasse and Fuggerstrasse especially) has been a gay mecca since the 1920s. Institutions like Tom's, Hafen and Connection pull in the punters nightly, and there's also plenty of nocturnal action for the leather and fetish set. Current hipster central is Kreuzberg, which teems with party pens, especially along Oranienstrasse and Mehringdamm, though none are exclusively gay. Across the river, Friedrichshain has a couple of gay bars alongside gay fave Berghain/Panorama Bar and the hardcore Lab.oratory. Old East Berlin's pink hub Prenzlauer Berg has a few low-key cafes and hardcore cruising dens.

Party Spectrum

Berlin's gayscape ranges from mellow cafes, campy bars and cinemas to saunas, cruising areas, clubs with darkrooms and all-out sex venues. In fact, sex and sexuality are entirely everyday matters to the unshockable city folk and there are very few, if any, itches that can't be quite openly and legally scratched. As elsewhere, gay men have more options, but grrrrls – from lipstick lesbians to bad-ass dykes – won't feel left out either. Some of the best club nights are independent of venues and may move around. Check the websites or magazines for the latest scoop.

Queue for Berghain/Panorama Bar

Best Bars & Cafes

Roses A plush, pink, tacky, campy madhouse that's an essential stop on a lesbigay bar-hop. (p105)

Möbel Olfe Usually mixed but gays rule on Thursdays, lesbians on Tuesdays. (p104)

Himmelreich This '50s retro lounge is a Friedrichshain scene stalwart; women-only Tuesdays, 2-4-1 Wednesdays. (p125)

Best Clubs & Parties

Berghain Post-industrial techno-electro hellhole for studly queer bass junkies; with darkrooms. (p124)

GMF Glamtastic Sunday club with pretty people in stylish retro location. (p53)

Bassy Trash diva Chantal's 'House of Shame' parties on Thursdays run wild and wicked. (p137)

Monster Ronson's Ichiban Karaoke Wacky karaoke den with gay-geared party nights. (p125)

Worth a Trip

In a new location at a former brewery in Neukölln, queer party institution **SchwuZ** (030-5770 2270; www.schwuz.de; Rollbergstrasse 26; Wed-Sun; 104,167, S Rathaus Neukölln) is still the go-to spot for high-energy flirting and dancing. Different nightly parties (eg Madonna Mania, Partysane, Popkicker) draw different punters, so check what's on before heading out. Good for easing into the gay party scene.

Best Music & Performance

Berlin's performing arts scene is lively, edgy and the most varied in the German-speaking world. With three state-supported opera houses, five major orchestras – including the world-class Berliner Philharmoniker – scores of theatres, cinemas, cabarets and concert venues, you've got enough entertainment options to last you a lifetime.

Best Rock, Pop & Indie

Lido Old cinema that's great for catching tomorrow's headlines of the rock-indie-electro-pop persuasion. (p113)

Magnet Club Essential indie rock venue and new-artist incubator. (p111)

Astra Kulturhaus Clued-in bookers line up everything from big-name artists to electro swing parties. (p125)

Best Jazz & Blues

A-Trane Been-there-for-ever saloon famous for attracting big talent and legendary jam sessions. (p95)

Best Classical Music

Berliner Philharmonie 'Cathedral of sound' and home base of the Berliner Philharmoniker. (p69)

Konzerthaus Berlin Schinkel-built jewel on Gendarmenmarkt. (p38)

Best Cabaret

Chamäleon Varieté Acrobatics, artistry and sex appeal in an intimate former ballroom. (p84)

Bar Jeder Vernunft High-quality entertainment in glam art nouveau mirrored tent. (p95)

Friedrichstadtpalast Europe's largest revue theatre puts on sparkly Vegas-style shows. (p84)

☑ Top Tips

▶ Many theatres are closed on Mondays and in July and August.

▶ Tickets for the Philharmonie, Staatsoper and blockbuster concerts should be purchased far in advance.

▶ **Hekticket** (☎030-230 9930; www.hekticket.de; Karl-Liebknecht-Strasse 13; ⏰noon-8pm Mon-Sat; Ⓢ Alexanderplatz, Ⓤ Alexanderplatz) next to Berlin Carré, sells left-over tickets for same-day performances at half price between 2pm and 7pm.

Best Quiet Spots

If your head is spinning with all the stimulus Berlin is throwing at you, there are plenty of places that can provide a restorative antidote. Fantastic outdoor spots and serene retreats lurk in every neighbourhood.

Best Parks & Gardens

Schlossgarten Charlottenburg Set up a picnic near the carp pond and ponder royal splendours. (p97)

Park Sanssouci Find your favourite spot away from the crowds in this sprawling royal park. (p139)

Best Cemeteries

Alter Jüdischer Friedhof Berlin's oldest Jewish cemetery was destroyed by the Nazis. (p81)

Jüdischer Friedhof Schönhauser Allee Final resting place of the painter Max Liebermann and other prominent Berlin Jews. (p133)

Best Memorial Sites

Neue Wache An antiwar memorial centred on an emotional Käthe Kollwitz sculpture. (p33)

Holocaust Memorial An outsized maze of stelae represents this outsized crime against humanity. (p28)

Luftbrückendenkmal Pay tribute to a true 'triumph of the will' at the Berlin Airlift Memorial. (p71)

Best Churches

Berliner Dom Royal court church cutting a commanding presence on Museum Island. (p49)

ARTIST: THREE GIRLS AND A BOY BY WILFRIED FITZENREITER; IMAGE: TONY C FRENCH/GETTY IMAGES ©

☑ Top Tips

▶ Get lost amid the restful expanse of lawns, trees and paths of the enormous **Tiergarten** (admission free; 🚌100, 200, S Brandenburger Tor, U Potsdamer Platz, Brandenburger Tor), Berlin's answer to London's Hyde Park or New York's Central Park. It's a beloved retreat from the city bustle, sprinkled with monuments, beer gardens and cultural sites.

Best With Kids

Travelling to Berlin with kids can be child's play, especially if you keep a light schedule and involve them in the day-to-day planning. There's plenty to keep the youngsters occupied, from zoos to kid-oriented museums to magic and puppet shows. Parks and imaginative playgrounds abound in all neighbourhoods, as do public pools.

Legoland Discovery Centre (☎01806 6669 0110; www.legolanddiscoverycentre.de/berlin; Potsdamer Strasse 4; admission €14-18.50; ⏰10am-7pm, last admission 5pm; 🚌200, S Potsdamer Platz, U Potsdamer Platz) The milk-tooth set delights in this indoor Lego wonderland with a 4D cinema, a Lego 'factory', a Dragon Castle 'slow-lercoaster' ride and a mini-Berlin with Lego-built landmarks.

Museum für Naturkunde See giant dinos come to life, travel through space to the beginning of time, find out why zebras are striped and get an eyeful of a giant housefly. (p79)

Science Center Spectrum (www.sdtb.de; Möckernstrasse 26; ⏰9am-5.30pm Tue-Fri, 10am-6pm Sat & Sun; S Möckernbrücke, Gleisdreieck) Toddlers to teens get to play, experience and learn about such concepts as balance, weight, water, air and electricity while pushing buttons, pulling levers and otherwise engaging in dozens of hands-on experiments.

Berlin Zoo If the 20,000 furry, feathered and finned friends fail to enchant the little ones, the adventure playground most likely will. (p90)

Madame Tussauds Kids of any age are all smiles when posing with the waxen likeness of their favourite pop star or celluloid celebrity. (p35)

Mauermuseum Teens with an interest in history and a decent attention span may enjoy the ingenious homemade contraptions used to escape from East Germany. (p66)

Computerspiele-museum (☎030-6098 8577; www.computerspiele-museum.de; Karl-Marx-Allee 93a; adult/concession €8/5; ⏰10am-8pm Wed-Mon; S Weberwiese) Older kids will get their kicks in this universe of computer games, from Pac-Man to World of Warcraft.

Deutsches Technik-museum (☎030-902 540; www.sdtb.de; Trebbiner Strasse 9; adult/concession €6/3, after 3pm under 18 free; ⏰9am-5.30pm Tue-Fri, 10am-6pm Sat & Sun; S Gleisdreieck) This giant shrine to technology counts the world's first computer, an entire hall of vintage locomotives and extensive exhibits on aviation and navigation.

Survival Guide

Survival Guide

Before You Go

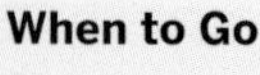

When to Go

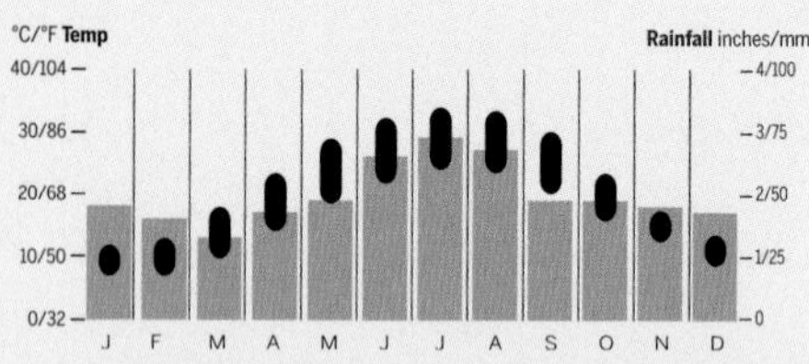

➡ **Winter (Nov–Feb)** Cold and dark, snow possible. Sights are crowd-free, theatre and concert season in full swing.

➡ **Spring (Mar–May)** Mild, often sunny. Sights start getting busier; festival season kicks off; beer gardens and outdoor cafes open.

➡ **Summer (Jun–Aug)** Warm to hot, often sunny, thunderstorms possible. Peak tourist season; sights and museums are super-busy; life moves outdoors.

➡ **Autumn (Sep–Oct)** Mild, often sunny. Theatre, concert and football (soccer) seasons start up.

Book Your Stay

☑ **Top Tip** To minimise travel time, avoid staying in a hotel outside the S-Bahn ring.

➡ With more hotel beds than New York, competition is fierce among Berlin properties and prices are low compared to other capital cities.

➡ The most central district is Mitte. Hotels around Kurfürstendamm are plentiful and close to the trade fairgrounds, but put you a U-Bahn ride away from most blockbuster sights and happening nightlife.

➡ Kreuzberg and Friedrichshain are ideal districts for party animals

➡ Berlin has a vibrant hostel scene with dorm beds starting at just €9 per night.

➡ Budget designer hotels with chic interiors but minimal amenities are all the rage.

➡ Nostalgic types should check into an old-fashioned

B&B, called *Hotel-Pension* or simply *Pension*; most prevalent in western districts, especially around Kurfürstendamm.

- Furnished flats are a popular alternative to hotels.
- Seasonal room-rate variations are rare but prices spike during major trade shows, festivals and public holidays.
- Reservations are essential around major holidays, cultural events and trade shows.
- Many properties set aside rooms or entire floors for nonsmokers.

Useful Websites

Lonely Planet (www.lonelyplanet.com/germany/berlin/hotels) Lonely Planet's online booking service with insider low-down on the best places to stay.

Visit Berlin (www.visitberlin.de) Official tourist authority.

Berlin30 (www.berlin30.com) Specialises in accommodation costing less than €30 per person.

Best Budget

EastSeven Berlin Hostel (www.eastseven.de) Small and delightful hostel close to hip hang-outs and public transport.

Grand Hostel Berlin (www.grandhostel-berlin.de) Historic lair blending character with modern comforts and amenities.

Meininger City Hostels Kreuzberg (www.meininger-hostels.de) Hotel-hostel combo with a comfort level to rival budget hotels.

Motel One Berlin-Alexanderplatz (www.motel-one.de) This budget designer chain is an excellent choice for those who value location over luxury.

Best Midrange

Circus Hotel (www.circus-berlin.de) Our favourite budget boutique hotel: unique mod rooms with thoughtful design details and quality beds.

Hotel Amano (www.amanogroup.de) Affordable designer hotel with inviting public areas and efficiently styled rooms.

Michelberger Hotel (www.michelbergerhotel.com) The ultimate in creative crash pads, perfectly encapsulating Berlin's offbeat DIY spirit.

25hours Hotel Bikini Berlin (www.25hours-hotels.com) 'Urban jungle'–themed hip lifestyle outpost.

Hotel Askanischer Hof (www.askanischer-hof.de) Character and vintage flair with a Roaring Twenties pedigree.

Ackselhaus & Blue Home (www.ackselhaus.de) Charismatic retreat in 19th-century building.

Best Top End

Das Stue (www.das-stue.com) This delightful refuge from the urban bustle has understated grandeur and the Tiergarten park as front yard.

Hotel Adlon Kempinski (www.kempinski.com) The full symphony of luxury in spacious, amenity-laden rooms and suites with timelessly regal decor.

Mandala Hotel (www.the-mandala.de) Swish cocoon of sophistication and unfussy ambience.

Casa Camper (www.casacamper.com) Plenty of design cachet, day-lit bathrooms, and lounge with free breakfast and refreshments, in Scheunenviertel.

Short-Stay Apartments

Miniloft Berlin (www.miniloft.com) Eight stunning lofts in an architect-converted building, with modern designer furniture and kitchenettes.

Brilliant Apartments (www.brilliant-apartments.de) Stylish and modern units with full kitchens and neat historic touches; some have a balcony.

T&C Apartments (www.tc-apartments-berlin.de) Huge selection of stylish, hand-picked apartments.

Arriving in Berlin

☑ **Top Tip** For the best way to get to your accommodation, see p17.

Berlin-Tegel Airport

➡ The TXL express bus connects Tegel to Alexanderplatz (€2.60, tariff AB; 40 minutes) via Hauptbahnhof (central train station) and Unter den Linden every 10 minutes.

➡ Bus X9 goes to Kurfürstendamm (€2.60, tariff AB; 20 minutes) every 10 minutes.

➡ The closest U-Bahn station is Jakob-Kaiser-Platz, served from Tegel by bus 109 and X9. From here, the U7 runs to Schöneberg and Kreuzberg. Trips cost €2.60 (tariff AB).

➡ Bus X9 connects Tegel with the closest S-Bahn station at Jungfernheide, a stop on the S41/S42 (Ringbahn, or circle line).

➡ Taxis cost about €20 to Zoologischer Garten and €25 to Alexanderplatz and take 30 to 45 minutes. A €0.50 surcharge applies to trips from Tegel.

Berlin-Schönefeld Airport

➡ Airport-Express trains make the 30-minute trip to central Berlin twice hourly. Note: these are regular regional trains denoted as RE7 and RB14 in timetables.

➡ The slower S-Bahn S9 runs every 20 minutes and is useful if you're headed to Friedrichshain (eg Ostkreuz, 30 minutes) or Prenzlauer Berg (eg Schönhauser Allee, 45 minutes).

➡ The train station is about 400m from the terminals. Free shuttle buses run every 10 minutes; walking takes five to 10 minutes.

➡ For all rides you need a tariff ABC transport ticket (€3.20).

➡ Taxi rides average €40 and take 40 minutes to an hour.

Berlin Brandenburg Airport

➡ At press time, no opening date had been set for the much-delayed new central airport. Check www.berlin-airport.de for the latest.

Hauptbahnhof

➡ Berlin's central train station is served by buses, trams, the S-Bahn and the U-Bahn.

➡ Taxi ranks are located out the north exit (Europaplatz) and south exit (Washingtonplatz). Expect to pay about €14 to Alexanderplatz, €13 to Zoologischer Garten.

ZOB (Central Coach Station)

➡ Most coaches arrive at the **Zentraler Omnibusbahnhof** (ZOB; ☎030-302 5361; www.iob-berlin.de; Masenallee 4-6; S Kaiserdamm) ear the trade fairgrounds the western city edge.

The closest U-Bahn sta-on, about 400m north, served by the handy 2, which runs straight rough the city centre.

The nearest S-Bahn ation is Messe Süd/ C about 200m east and rved by the S41/S42 ngbahn (circle line), andy for Prenzlauer erg, Friedrichshain and eukölln.

➡ Taxi rides cost about €14 to the western city centre and €23 to Alexanderplatz.

Getting Around

U-Bahn

☑ **Best for...** Getting around Berlin quickly.

➡ U-Bahn lines are designated as U1, U2 etc.

➡ Trains operate from 4am until about 12.30am and all night Friday, Saturday and public holidays (all lines except U4 and U55).

➡ From Sunday through Thursday, night buses (designated N2, N5 etc) follow the U-Bahn routes between 12.30am and 4am every 30 minutes.

➡ For information and trip planning, see www.bvg.de.

Tickets & Passes

➡ The public transport network is operated by **BVG** (☎030-194 49; www.bvg.de).

➡ One ticket is good on all forms of public transport. Most trips within Berlin require an AB ticket (€2.60), valid for two hours (interruptions and transfers allowed, round trips not). Trips to Potsdam and Schönefeld Airport require an ABC ticket (€3.60).

➡ The short-trip ticket (*Kurzstreckentarif*; €1.50) is valid for three stops on any U-Bahn or S-Bahn or six stops on any bus or tram.

➡ Children aged six to 14 qualify for reduced *(ermässigt)* rates, while kids under six travel free.

➡ One-day travel passes *(Tageskarte)* are valid for unlimited travel on all forms of public transport until 3am the next day. The AB zone is €6.70. Group day passes *(Kleingruppenkarte)* for up to five people travelling together cost €16.20.

➡ Buy tickets from vending machines in U- or S-Bahn stations and aboard trams, from bus drivers and at station offices and news kiosks sporting the yellow BVG logo. Don't buy tickets from scammers selling used ones outside stations. Some vending machines accept debit cards. Bus drivers and tram vending machines only take cash.

➡ Single tickets, except those bought from bus drivers and in trams, must be stamped before boarding. Getting caught without a valid ticket incurs a €40 fine payable on the spot.

S-Bahn

☑ **Best for...** Covering longer distances within Berlin.

➡ S-Bahn trains make fewer stops than the U-Bahn. Denoted as S1, S2 etc, they operate from 4am to 12.30am and all night on Friday, Saturday and public holidays.

➡ Full details at www.s-bahn-berlin.de.

Bus

☑ **Best for...** City sightseeing on the cheap.

➡ City buses run frequently between 4.30am and 12.30am.

➡ Half-hourly night buses take over in the interim.

➡ MetroBuses, designated M19, M41 etc, operate 24/7.

➡ Buses 100 and 200 follow routes linking major sights.

➡ For information, see www.bvg.de.

Tram

☑ **Best for...** Covering neighbourhoods not served by other transport.

➡ Trams only operate in the eastern districts.

➡ Trams designated M1, M2 etc run 24/7.

Bicycle

☑ **Best for...** Exploring local neighbourhoods.

➡ Many hostels and hotels have guest bicycles.

➡ Rental stations abound and range from kiosks and petrol stations to bike shops and bike ranks.

➡ The websites www.bbbike.de and www.vmz-info.de are handy for route planning.

➡ With a *Fahrradkarte* (bicycle ticket, €1.70), bicycles may be taken aboard designated U-Bahn and S-Bahn carriages (usually the first and last ones; look for the bicycle logo).

Taxi

☑ **Best for...** Late nights and groups sharing the cost.

➡ Taxis can be ordered by phone (☎030-443 322 or ☎030-210 202), flagged down or picked up at a rank.

➡ Flag fall is €3.40, then it's €1.79 per kilometre up to 7km and €1.28 for each additional kilometre.

➡ The short-trip rate (*Kurzstreckentarif*) lets you ride for up to 2km for a mere €4, but only if you flag down a moving taxi and request this rat[e] before the driver has ac[ti]vated the regular meter.

➡ Tip about 10%.

Essential Informatio[n]

Business Hours

☑ **Top Tip** Many boutiques and smaller shop[s] don't open until noon an[d] close at 6pm or 7pm.

Bars 6pm to 1am or late[r]

Clubs 11pm to 5am or later

Restaurants 11am to 10.30pm

Shops 10am to 8pm Mon-Sat

Discount Cards

☑ **Top Tip** The Museumspass Berlin bu[ys] admission to the permanent exhibits of about 50 museums on three consecutive opening day[s]. It sells for €24 (concession €12) at Berlin touris[t] offices and participating museums.

Berlin Welcome Card (www.berlin-welcomecard.de) Entitles you to unlimite[d] public transport and up

50% discount on 200 ghts, attractions and urs for periods of two, ree or five days.

tyTourCard (www. ytourcard.com) Unlimited blic transport and a inimum 15% discount 40 partner sights, tractions and tours, for o, three or five days.

lectricity

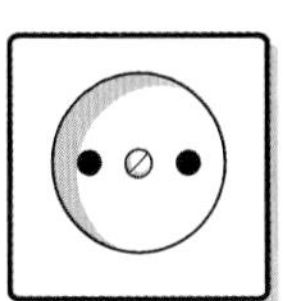

230V/50Hz

mergency

re Department (☎112)

lice (☎110)

oney

Top Tip The easiest y to obtain cash is from ATM *(Geldautomat)* linked to international networks like Cirrus, Plus, Star and Maestro. Check with your bank for fees and daily withdrawal limits.

➡ The German currency is the euro (€), divided into 100 cents.

➡ Cash is king in Berlin; credit cards are not as widely used as in other countries. Always enquire first.

➡ Report lost or stolen cards at ☎116 116.

Public Holidays

Neujahrstag (New Year's Day) 1 January

Ostern (Easter; Good Friday, Easter Sunday and Easter Monday) late March/April

Christi Himmelfahrt (Ascension Day) 40 days after Easter, always on a Thursday

Maifeiertag (May Day) 1 May

Pfingsten (Whit/ Pentecost Sunday and Monday) May/June

Tag der Deutschen Einheit (Unification Day) 3 October

Weihnachten (Christmas Day, Boxing Day) 25–26 December

Telephone

➡ Berlin's city code is ☎030; Germany's country code is ☎49.

➡ Mobile (cell) phones (*Handys* in German)

Late-Night & Sunday Shopping

➡ One handy feature of Berlin culture is the *Spätkauf* (*Späti* in local vernacular), which are small neighbourhood stores stocked with the basics and open from early evening until 2am or later.

➡ Some supermarkets (especially select branches of the Kaiser's chain) stay open until midnight; a few even through the night.

➡ Shops and supermarkets in major train stations (Hauptbahnhof, Ostbahnhof, Friedrichstrasse) are open late and on Sundays.

➡ Petrol stations also stock some basic supplies, though usually at inflated prices.

operate on GSM900/1800. If your home country uses a different standard, you'll need a multiband GSM phone in Germany. Check roaming charges with your provider or buy an international plan.

➡ If you have an unlocked phone that works in Germany, buying a prepaid, rechargeable local SIM card (eg at Netto, Aldi or Lidl supermarkets) may bring costs down.

Toilets

☑ **Top Tip** Men can have a quaint pee in the octagonal Christmas-tree-green *pissoirs* that are vestiges from the 19th century, when indoor plumbing was less commonplace.

➡ Free-standing pay toilet pods are scattered throughout central Berlin.

➡ Toilets in malls, department stores, public venues, cafes and restaurants are often attended by cleaners who either charge a fee (usually €0.50) or expect a small tip.

Tourist Information

The local tourist board, **Visit Berlin** (www.visitberlin.de), operates a handful of walk-in offices and a **call centre** (☎030-250 025; ⌚9am-7pm Mon-Fri, 10am-6pm Sat, 10am-2pm Sun) whose multilingual staff field general questions and make hotel and ticket bookings. Some useful locations:

Hauptbahnhof (Europaplatz entrance, ground fl; ⌚8am-10pm; S Hauptbahnhof, U Hauptbahnhof)

Brandenburg Gate (Map p30, D3; Pariser Platz; ⌚9.30am-7pm Apr-Oct, to 6pm Nov-Mar; S Brandenburger Tor, U Brandenburger Tor)

TV Tower (Map p48, D2; ground fl; ⌚10am-6pm Apr-Oct, to 4pm Nov-Mar; 🚌100, 200, S Alexanderplatz, U Alexanderplatz)

Neues Kranzler Eck (Map p88, E2) Kurfürstendamm 22; ⌚9.30am-8pm Mon-Sat; S Kurfürstendamm)

Travellers with Disabilities

➡ There are access ramps and/or lifts in many public buildings, including train stations, museums, concert halls and cinemas.

➡ Numerous buses and trams are wheelchair-accessible and many U- and S-Bahn stations are equipped with ramps or lifts. Many stations also have grooved platforms to assist vision-impaired passengers.

Dos & Don'ts

➡ Do say '*Guten Tag*' when entering a business.

➡ Do state your last name at the start of a phone call.

➡ Do bring a small gift or flowers when invited to a home-cooked meal.

➡ Do bag your own groceries in supermarkets. And quickly!

➡ Don't be late for appointments and dinner invitations.

➡ Don't talk about WWII with a victor's mentality.

➡ Don't assume you can pay by credit card, especially when eating out.

For trip-planning as-
sistance, contact **BVG**
(030-19449; www.bvg.de).

Rollstuhlpannendienst
(0177 833 5773; www.
llstuhlpannendienst.de)
rovides 24-hour wheel-
hair repairs and offers
heelchair rentals.

Visas

➡ Most EU nationals need only their national identity card or passport to enter Germany.

➡ Australian, Canadian, Israeli, Japanese, New Zealand, Swiss and US citizens need only a valid passport (no visa) for tourist stays under three months.

➡ Nationals from most other countries must apply for a Schengen visa with the consulate of the Schengen country that is your primary destination.

➡ For full details and the latest regulations, see www.auswaertiges-amt.de or check with a German consulate in your country.

Language

It's easy to pronounce German because almost all sounds are also found in English – just read our pronunciation guides as if they were English and you'll be understood.

In German, word stress falls mostly on the first syllable – in our pronunciation guides the stressed syllable is indicated with italics.

Note that German has polite and informal forms for 'you' (*Sie* and *du* respectively). When addressing people you don't know well, use the polite form. In this language guide, polite forms are used, unless you see (pol/inf) which indicates we've given both options. Also note that (m/f) indicates masculine and feminine forms.

To enhance your trip with a phrasebook, visit **lonelyplanet.com**.

Basics

Hello.
Guten Tag. — *goo*·ten taak

Goodbye.
Auf Wiedersehen. — owf *vee*·der·zey·en

How are you? (pol/inf)
Wie geht es Ihnen/dir? — vee gayt es *ee*·nen/deer

Fine, thanks.
Danke, gut. — *dang*·ke goot

Please.
Bitte. — *bi*·te

Thank you.
Danke. — *dang*·ke

Excuse me.
Entschuldigung. — ent·*shul*·di·gung

Sorry.
Entschuldigung. — ent·*shul*·di·gung

Yes./No.
Ja./Nein. — yah/nain

Do you speak (English)?
Sprechen Sie Englisch? — *shpre*·khen zee *eng*·lish

I (don't) understand.
Ich verstehe (nicht). — ikh fer·*shtay*·e (nikht)

Eating & Drinking

I'm a vegetarian. (m/f)
Ich bin Vegetarier/ Vegetarierin. — ikh bin ve·ge·*tah*·ri·er/ ve·ge·*tah*·ri·e·in

Cheers!
Prost! — prawst

That was delicious!
Das war sehr lecker! — das vahr zair *le*·ker

Please bring the bill.
Die Rechnung, bitte. — dee *rekh*·nung *bi*·te

I'd like ...
Ich möchte ... — ikh *merkh*·te ...

a coffee	*einen Kaffee*	*ai*·nen *ka*·fay
a glass of wine	*ein Glas Wein*	ain glas wain
a table for two	*einen Tisch für zwei Personen*	*ai*·nen tish für tsvai per·*zaw*·nen
two beers	*zwei Bier*	tsvai beer

Shopping

I'd like to buy ...
Ich möchte ... kaufen. — ikh *merkh*·te ... *kow*·fen

ay I look at it?
önnen Sie es ir zeigen? — *ker*·nen zee es meer *tsai*·gen

ow much is it?
ie viel kostet das? — vee feel *kos*·tet das

hat's too expensive.
as ist zu teuer. — das ist tsoo *toy*·er

an you lower the price?
önnen Sie mit em Preis eruntergehen? — *ker*·nen zee mit dem prais he·*run*·ter·gay·en

here's a mistake in the bill.
a ist ein Fehler in er Rechnung. — dah ist ain *fay*·ler in dair *rekh*·nung

mergencies

elp!
ilfe! — *hil*·fe

all a doctor!
ufen Sie nen Arzt! — *roo*·fen zee *ai*·nen artst

all the police!
ufen Sie ie Polizei! — *roo*·fen zee dee po·li·*tsai*

m lost.
h habe ich verirrt. — ikh *hah*·be mikh fer·*irt*

m ill.
h bin krank. — ikh bin krangk

here's the toilet?
o ist die Toilette? — vo ist dee to·a·*le*·te

ime & Numbers

hat time is it?
ie spät ist es? — vee shpayt ist es

's (10) o'clock.
s ist (zehn) Uhr. — es ist (tsayn) oor

orning	*Morgen*	*mor*·gen
fternoon	*Nachmittag*	*nahkh*·mi·tahk
vening	*Abend*	*ah*·bent
yesterday	*gestern*	*ges*·tern
today	*heute*	*hoy*·te
tomorrow	*morgen*	*mor*·gen

1	*eins*	ains
2	*zwei*	tsvai
3	*drei*	*drai*
4	*vier*	feer
5	*fünf*	fünf
6	*sechs*	zeks
7	*sieben*	zee·ben
8	*acht*	akht
9	*neun*	noyn
10	*zehn*	tsayn
100	*hundert*	*hun*·dert
1000	*tausend*	*tow*·sent

Transport & Directions

Where's ...?
Wo ist ...? — vaw ist ...

What's the address?
Wie ist die Adresse? — vee ist dee a·*dre*·se

Can you show me (on the map)?
Können Sie es mir (auf der Karte) zeigen? — *ker*·nen zee es meer (owf dair *kar*·te) *tsai*·gen

I want to go to ...
Ich mochte nach ... fahren. — ikh *merkh*·te nahkh ... *fah*·ren

What time does it leave?
Wann fährt es ab? — van fairt es ap

What time does it arrive?
Wann kommt es an? — van komt es an

Does it stop at ...?
Hält es in ...? — helt es in ...

I want to get off here.
Ich mochte hier aussteigen. — ikh *merkh*·te heer *ows*·shtai·gen

Behind the Scenes

Send Us Your Feedback

We love to hear from travellers – your comments help make our books better. We read every word, and we guarantee that your feedback goes straight to the authors. Visit **lonelyplanet.com/contact** to submit your updates and suggestions.

Note: We may edit, reproduce and incorporate your comments in Lonely Planet products such as guidebooks, websites and digital products, so let us know if you don't want your comments reproduced or your name acknowledged. For a copy of our privacy policy visit lonelyplanet.com/privacy.

Our Readers

Many thanks to the travellers who used the last edition and wrote to us: Bernard Clark, Charlie Gatehouse, Dan Dutfield, Ed Loh, Jan O'Brien, Jenny Wystawnoha, Katrin Flatscher, Majken Irene Nielsen, Michael Vivian-Lewis, Miladin Bogetic, Norman Cohen, Pauline Simpson, Sarah Bennett & Lee Slater, Sarah Hooper, Taly Matiteyahu

Andrea Schulte-Peevers' Thanks

Big heartfelt thanks to all these wonderful people (in no particular order): Henrik Tidefjärd, Susan Paterson, Miriam Bers, Claudia Scheffler, Regine Schneider, Frank Engster, Heiner & Claudia Schuster, Renate Freiling, Silke Neumann, Kirsten Schmidt, Christian Tänzler, Julia Ana Herchenbach, Johann Scharfe, Shachar & Doreen Elkanati, Ariela Abramovici-Dähne, Craig Robinson, Ubin Eoh, Mike Meinke, Virginia Shmuel, Jan Czyszke and David Peevers.

Acknowledgments

Cover photograph: Norman Forster's Reichstag Dome, travelstock44/Alamy

This Book

This 4th edition of Lonely Planet's *Pocket Berlin* was researched and written by Andrea Schulte-Peevers; she also wrote the previous two editions. This guidebook was commissioned in Lonely Planet's London office and produced by the following: **Commissioning Editor** Anna Tyler **Destination Editor** Gemma Graham **Coordinating Editor** Kirsten Rawlings **Product Editor** Penny Cordner **Senior Cartographer** Valentina Kremenchutskaya **Book Designer** Clara Monitto **Assisting Editor** Gabrielle Stefanos **Assisting Book Designer** Wibowo Rusli **Cover Researcher** Naomi Parker **Thanks to** Ryan Evans, Larissa Frost, Anna Harris, Jouve India, Claire Naylor, Karyn Noble, Katie O'Connell, Ellie Simpson, Tony Wheeler

ndex

See also separate subindexes for:

Eating p187
Drinking p188
Entertainment p188
Shopping p188

Sights 000
Map Pages **000**

Eating

Drinking

Entertainmer

Shopping

Our Writer

Andrea Schulte-Peevers

Born and raised in Germany and educated in London and at UCLA, Andrea has travelled the distance to the moon and back in her visits to some 75 countries, but her favourite place in the world is still Berlin. She's written about her native country for two decades and authored or contributed to some 80 Lonely Planet titles, including all editions of this guide, the *Berlin* city guide, the *Germany* country guide and the *Discover Germany* guide.

Published by Lonely Planet Publications Pty Ltd
ABN 36 005 607 983
4th edition – Feb 2015
ISBN 978 1 74220 881 7

10 9 8 7 6 5
Printed in China